It is my pleasure to present the newest book from John Burdett, "My Homework Ate The Dog – Leadership in an Upside Down World"

We are privileged to have John as Bedford's Leadership advisor and I believe you will find this book helpful in your organization's quest for excellence.

BEDFORD
inspiring leaders to choose **you**

MY HOMEWORK ATE THE DOG

THE PATH TO MASTERY

MY HOMEWORK ATE THE DOG

Leadership in an UPSIDE-DOWN WORLD

John O. Burdett

MY HOMEWORK ATE THE DOG

© Orxestra Inc., 2011

ISBN 978-0-9687233-6-4
National Library of Canada Cataloguing

Published by
Executive Forum, a division of Canada Forum Inc.
Toronto, Ontario

Individual and bulk orders can be placed:
By phone: (416) 925-0866
By email: info@canadaforum.com

Printed in Canada

www.orxestra.com

Today's business is a steeplechase

The world doesn't look as it did at the turn of this century. Terrorism, a financial meltdown, the crash of the housing market, the pre-eminence of China, the emergence of India as an economic powerhouse, a black US President, the social networking phenomenon, product as art (Apple), the boomers moving out and a new generational cohort moving in – taken together, these developments describe not just a changed world, but one that has been turned upside down.

History doesn't repeat itself – people do. To survive is to adapt; it's to recognize that those who adapt the fastest are the ones who will be around the longest. In the recent past, business could be likened to a 10,000-metre race: it was all about tactics and stamina. Today's business is a steeplechase; when you come to the inevitable water jump, simply running harder won't keep you in the race.

The title of the book speaks to the upside-down nature of today's business environment. Not made explicit, but an essential point nevertheless, is that things are not going to go back to the way they were. Those sitting on the sidelines assuming the familiar will return will be waiting a long time.

The book is in four parts

My Homework Ate the Dog explores four pivotal dimensions of today's leadership challenge: (Part one) Getting middle managers back in the game; (Part two) Taking the team to the next level; (Part three) Engaging the heart, enriching the spirit; and (Part four) Measuring culture. In today's upside-down world, we strongly suggest that if organizations are found lacking in any one of these dimensions, failure doesn't beckon – it screams out in full Dolby surround sound: "Run this way!"

With an action bias in mind, the next steps suggested in each chapter are neither the realm of the highly conceptual nor exclusively the province of those planning what they need to do differently a year from now. The audience is the practising manager. The suggestions and ideas are all about what the reader can start to do differently on Monday! To best draw out those next steps, and recognizing that without reflection there is no learning, each chapter concludes with a series of key questions. Consider working through those questions with your team.

Unbundling the content

Part one emphasizes that no matter what some may suggest, middle managers are still the most important resource any organization has. *Chapter one* looks at why organizations need to get those in the middle back in the game. *Chapter two* outlines why, more than ever, leadership means cultivating the grapevine. *Chapter three* explores the statement, "If you are not managing your culture, someone else is!" Here a brief word about Chapter one. It was deliberately written to be provocative – to get your attention. You may feel that the comments made about middle managers do not apply to your business. That may be, but we would suggest you get into the middle of the organization and test that assumption before dismissing the ideas out of hand.

Part two revisits a well-worn theme: the team. The content here, however, is far more than just a matter of old wine in new bottles. Today, any leader who thinks about succeeding without a great support team has a fool for an advisor. The agile organization forms that are emerging, the emphasis on business partnerships, and the influence of networking technology – all put a new emphasis on what it means to be a "team." *Chapter four* focuses on a leadership paradox: You can't change the team by trying to change the team. *Chapter five* describes practical ways to take the team to the next level of performance. A hint here – it's not about teambuilding! *Chapter six* lays out the steps involved in delivering masterful coaching. And *Chapter seven* visits a skill that in many organizations is a lost art: the tough conversation.

Part three is all about leadership. Two generations of business school trained leaders have been strongly influenced by a leadership approach dominated by addressing the head (strategy) and delivering the hand (strategic implementation). What all too often has been left out of the leadership weave are the human qualities needed to engage and inspire. What has often been given a second order of priority is how successful leaders engage the heart and enrich the spirit. When the ground ahead is fraught with risk ... it matters for naught if you have a great plan of attack, that your weaponry is superior, that you are the first to leap over the parapet – if the rest of the troops don't follow. Part three focuses on the role that humility plays in today's leadership *(Chapter eight)*; why to lead is to listen *(Chapter nine)*; caring as a way of life *(Chapter ten)*; and why "catching people doing it right" is a leadership imperative *(Chapter eleven)*.

Part four develops the theme "What you measure is what you get." Based on the author's work on organization learning going back to the mid-nineties, *Chapter twelve* outlines the relationship between learning and culture. Endorsing the action bias theme, the final part of the book introduces the "Culture Work-Up." This is a simple, unique, and in its own way a compelling assessment of (1) the organization's culture today and (2) the culture the organization needs (not wants) moving forward. Investing time in the "Culture Work-Up" provides a platform for all of the leadership actions described in the book.

The source of the ideas

In reviewing the book's content, the reader may ask where the ideas and suggestions come from. Over the past decade and a half, I have consulted in over 25 countries with some of the world's best-known organizations and with leaders whose names, in some instances, make headlines in the international business press. In recent years, however, I have become especially interested in the plight of middle managers. This has involved dozens of workshops and seminars (in both the Private and Public sectors and involving public workshops and in-house programs) with, literally, many hundreds of those who inhabit the middle rungs of the organization. The conversation in those workshops, the questions that come up, the success stories, and the suggestions that emerge underpin this book. Ongoing coaching of a small cadre of CEOs, dialogue with peers, and my consulting work around organization culture add to the ideas presented.

Each chapter is standalone

This is my fifth book in the past decade. One of the practical aspects of each of those books is that any single chapter can be read without having to digest earlier parts of the book. This simple idea has been strongly endorsed by a number of readers. Time is at a premium. Some ideas resonate more strongly with one particular leader than with another. Presenting the book this way recognizes that effective leaders manage their time judiciously.

The general idea is that (1) each chapter contains a complete idea; (2) the chapters can thus be read in any order; and (3) any chapter can be enjoyed during a one-hour plane journey. A small trade-off in this publishing philosophy is that occasionally it becomes necessary to revisit key points made in an earlier chapter.

Enjoy the book. You are invited to dip into the content as and where you feel that the ideas and suggestions support your own leadership journey. Take time to reflect on the questions posed. Involve your team in the conversation. Focus on what you can do on Monday morning that would make the greatest difference. And remember, if it isn't written down, it won't happen!

Contents

Part one:
GETTING MIDDLE MANAGERS BACK IN THE GAME

"The reports of my death are greatly exaggerated."
— *Mark Twain*

Chapter one:
RE-ENGAGING THE MIDDLE KINGDOM

In an upside-down world

The modern organization is built on several basic beliefs:

> ❯ Its reason to be is to create tomorrow's customer.
> ❯ Shareholders can and should expect a fair return.
> ❯ Hierarchy in some form is inevitable.
> ❯ Management and ownership are not necessarily the same thing.
> ❯ Every business is potentially a growth business.
> ❯ The ongoing success of any enterprise rests heavily on a relatively small cadre of managers in the middle.

Not unlike non-commissioned officers in the military, middle managers have always taken pride in the conviction that they were an essential and loyal resource. Not so today. Ask for candid input from those who inhabit the middle reaches of the organization, and you will find that many of them feel distraught, disappointed, downtrodden, and worst of all, disenfranchised.

The narrative of the trapped mind

"We value middle managers. We want to take advantage of their potential contribution, but right now it's difficult to know how to actually do that."

"To be honest, many of our middle managers have settled in for retirement."

"There's a big gap between the attitude and approach of middle managers and the young people we are now hiring. It's not easy to see where and how we can bridge that gap."

"We really don't expect middle managers to act as or take on the mantle of a leader. Their main (only) role is to push for day-to-day results."

"Work–life balance is a laudable concept, but who it was that came up with that idea has never worked around here."

The rest of the story …

When the game changes, it changes for everyone.

3

Re-engaging the Middle Kingdom

"When middle managers no longer care, front-line employees no longer dare."

Before permanent settlements, before farming, before writing, the campfire was a source of comfort, a means to build camaraderie, and, no less important, an action learning classroom.

And just what did our hunter-gatherer kith-and-kin talk about as they enjoyed the unmatched security that fire represented? The ongoing challenge of community, sharing stories, and seeking an answer to life's mysteries have always been at the very centre of man's quest for meaning. Food, the hunt, the weather, the family, and a better tomorrow were also, no doubt, ever-popular topics.

It's fair to assume, however, that there was one theme – a life or death agenda – that could always be counted on to bring another log to the fire. That theme: leadership. The ever-present questions: Who was moving up? Who could be trusted? And above all else, who was the group willing to follow? Since man's beginnings in Africa, it was ever thus.

Fast-forward 50,000 years or so to a world not so different. Isn't strategy just another way to plan for the hunt? For market research, dwell on the primitive role of tracking. For the board meeting, write in "tribal council." For innovation and process improvement, consider how flint-making and husbandry evolved. For dialogue around who is ready to move up, consider the imperative that succession represents. For organization culture, read symbolism, ritual, myths, mores, and beliefs that established what was, and what wasn't, acceptable group behaviour. As for teamwork, think about what working together must have really meant when "collaborate or die" meant exactly that. And while "followership" may not literally be about life or death anymore, in organizational terms it's still very much about survival.

It's something of a mystery, therefore, why organizations[1] over the past decade or so have seemingly gone out of their way to disenfranchise the one group that shapes how followership thrives or perishes: We're talking about middle management. More specifically, why have many top leaders chosen to push to one side the growing alienation, frustration, cynicism and, yes, anger of those invaluable men and women in the middle? And make no mistake, a growing number of today's middle managers **are** becoming ever-more disillusioned, ever-more disheartened by the role they are being asked to play.

---

1   I do not have the research data to definitively capture the overall scope and scale of the middle management malaise outlined. Clearly, it's not all organizations. Indeed, I have clients where middle managers are flourishing. On the other hand, when one considers the total business landscape, I believe the alienation described is a real and growing concern.

It's not that those at the top of the house don't recognize the current malaise. It's not that they are unaware of the unprecedented fall-off in morale of those who have historically been the backbone of a successful organization. Perhaps the harsh truth is that not a few senior executives are of the mind that the middle manager – like the tiger, the river dolphin, and the lowland gorilla – is an endangered species and that the habitat that allowed them to flourish in the past can no longer support their existence.

The impending death of middle management

Decline, once underway, more often than not creates its own self-fulfilling downward momentum. Admiration for the grace, strength, and prowess of the polar bear doesn't mean it will survive. Although over half the Amazon rainforest – often referred to as the lungs of the planet – has already been stripped bare, that doesn't mean that a new beginning beckons. And just because middle managers are charged with what in past times was described as "a linchpin role,"[2] that doesn't mean they are following any kind of sustainable path.

Assuming a relatively flat structure, middle managers can be defined as those in roles two levels below the chief executives and one level above the front-line workers. Their demise, which some suggest as inevitable, can be traced to three key issues:

> *Decline, once underway, more often than not creates its own self-fulfilling downward momentum.*

(1) The separation of authority and knowledge

Since the early days of the Industrial Revolution, authority **and** knowledge have been pivotal to what it means to manage. They have provided a dual-footprint that year-in, year-out, lap after lap, has given middle managers the traction they needed to get things done through others. That is changing. Indeed, those once inseparable "twins" are going through a difficult and emotional separation.

Authority and knowledge is a well-choreographed song and dance act that got the proverbial "hook" when it became apparent that the first twelve months of a four-year degree in technology was redundant by the time the curtain came down on the final year. The relationship was recast the day an independent business in Israel became a part of your organization's research and design team. It was written anew

---

2   A term coined by Rensis Likert (1903–1981) describing those who serve as vital links between groups in successful organizations.

when Generation Y and their younger siblings started to bring a level of technical knowledge, computer literacy, and social media savvy to the job that the individual they reported to couldn't match.

Separating assumed authority from know-how changes the game. It reframes the cultural assumptions whereby influence, respect, and trust are distributed. It represents a potential shift of power – especially in a business built around technology – that, all too easily, can mean managing the technology gets more attention than managing the business.[3] Even the less virulent strains of this "techno-myopia" devalues "management" as a discipline. Middle managers – including those who built their career on past technological expertise – are, as a result, in danger of being cast in the role of administrator.

The obsolescence factor: Anyone who doubts the scope and limiting nature of a mindset that sees problems exclusively through a technological lens should think back to the events of April–June 2010. Literally thousands of the world's best experts were engaged in (1) stemming the flow of oil from the damaged British Petroleum oil rig in the Gulf of Mexico and (2) limiting the damage from the oil to the Louisiana coast.[4] As it happened, this profusion of experts failed with the first and largely overlooked the second. Of course, everything humanly possible was brought to the challenge, except, that is, effective management and its alter ego – inspired leadership.

(2) Ever-faster clock speed

When you can get new eyeglasses in under an hour, it shapes people's perception of responsiveness. Today, quality is assumed but speed kills – the competition, that is. The need to act fast, combined with an expanding range of channels to connect with the buyer, means the right person to make the decision is invariably the individual who deals directly with the customer. "I'll have to check with my supervisor" is the death knell of any service provider.

Building customer loyalty thus rests, in no small measure, on the degree of discretion enjoyed by those who interface directly with the buyer – be it a direct sales issue or a major project. Front-line responsiveness – and with it, the ability to make decisions close to the customer – rules the day.

The obsolescence factor: Pulling the middle manager into the loop impedes the speed

---

3 What we are describing is a form of techno-entitlement: "I am here for the technology, I want to be on the leading edge of technology, I want to revel in the technology ... Don't distract me with issues of how the business makes money. That's not what I am all about!"

4 The flow of oil stopped in mid-July 2010.

of response. Middle managers are, thus, not infrequently "the last to know." Those time-tested canons of front-line employee success, "no surprises" and "always make your leader-one-level-up look good," have been replaced by a "Nike-like" philosophy of "Just Do It!" Arguably, that's a good thing – as long as it's understood that when the culture changes at the sharp end of the business, you impact a whole lot of other behaviour – often in unanticipated ways.[5]

(3) Teaming

The team is the basic building block of the modern organization. For "teaming" read virtual teams, project teams, ad-hoc teams, process teams, product development teams, action learning teams, teams focusing on innovation, teams that work with customers and suppliers, etc.

When the crash of the falling pyramid drowns out plaintive cries of those hanging on grimly to the last vestiges of the status quo, when end-to-end processes dominate – the classical, hierarchical supervisory role gives way to a host of different team-leading challenges; opportunities where, in many instances, the team leader is not the individual to whom those sitting around the table are immediately responsible.

If you do the same old things in the same old way, you get the same old results. Breakthrough thinking, a step change, innovation, a new order of things, on the other hand, are invariably outcomes of unplanned disruption, a willingness to embrace paradox, a new question, or risk-taking by a creative individual who feels compelled to push against the grain.

Innovation is carried along on a stream of curiosity that rarely follows an established path. Traditional approaches to supervision emphasize order, control, established reporting relationships, and above all else, the need to ask permission. Letting go, pushing decision making close to the customer, and creating the space for people to play, aren't exactly writ large on the middle manager's job description.[6] And yet this is exactly what needs to happen if the default outcome for new ideas is other than that they quietly and inexorably morph into "what might have been."

The obsolescence factor: When any of us are threatened, the fight-or-flight instinct kicks in. For many middle managers, "fight" finds expression in moving into full command-and-control mode. It means first erecting and then moving behind a

---

5   Culture is a system – change one element and you impact the whole.

6   Knowing when to step back and, in doing so, create the space for new ideas to emerge vs. the assumption that being a manager is to "be in charge" is especially confusing for someone new to a middle management position.

barricade constructed from the rules, policies, procedures, and past precedents. "Flight" is to jettison the encouragement, affirmation, and emotional support needed if team members are to embrace risk. Flight is to let the cynics ("we already tried that") and naysayers ("that won't work here") dominate the airwaves. Either scenario – fight or flight – means the middle manager, with a good deal of justification, soon becomes labelled as an "innovation blocker."

James Watt didn't build the first steam engine (Thomas Newcomen did); Henry Ford didn't invent the assembly line (the idea had its origins in the nineteenth century); the Wright Brothers didn't make the first powered flight (although it was unpiloted, Samuel Pierpont Langley "flew" the first plane). Innovation is far more about building on the ideas of others than it is about being first (invention). Organizations are awash with ideas. What they also have in abundance are structures, protocols, procedures, processes, and assumptions about risk that often suffocate even the healthiest idea before it's strong enough to survive on its own.

> *Innovation is carried along on a stream of curiosity that rarely follows an established path.*

The shift from authority to influence, the culture changes wrought when speed enters the equation, the need for managers to work the context such that innovation flourishes – don't just change the way things get done – they amount to a new game. Decisions that in the past were the prerogative of one easy-to-identify individual are now likely reached through a subtle form of shared accountability. And the qualities demanded of those who are going to excel in the new game? Agility, resilience, speed, and comfort with ambiguity.[7]

This erosion of identity and, with it, uncertainty around contribution is compounded when middle managers lack genuine mastery in those things they are uniquely accountable for – when they are found wanting in the "Holy Trinity" of middle management performance effectiveness: (1) hiring, (2) employee development, and (3) performance management.

---

7   I return to this later in the chapter, under Tactic 7 – "Push for mastery in hiring" – where I suggest a more complete list of required competencies for today's middle manager.

Comfort with ambiguity

In many ways, this phrase defines the future of middle management. Groucho Marx once said that authenticity is the one thing you can't fake. He may well have been right, but comfort with ambiguity isn't too easy to fake either. Embracing ambiguity means being able to operate with little or no structure; moving forward without a detailed map; being willing to give up control; and being able to relate to that which lies outside of one's own experience. Knowledge of the topic, self-confidence, a natural curiosity, the joy of experimentation, being wedded to diversity, not taking oneself too seriously and a sense of humour, clearly, also play a role.

The problem is that, middle manager or not, there are those amongst us who are ill-equipped to deal with uncertainty – to grapple with variables that are difficult to define, arguments built around abstract concepts, contradictory points of view. Most problematic of all are those who are not yet ready to adopt a leadership approach dependent on collaboration.

Being a middle manager has always been a challenging role. Frustrating and at times exasperating, but with one saving grace – there was a degree of comfort drawn from knowing how tomorrow **would** unfold. It takes a different mindset and energy level to work in an environment where making it up as you go becomes an essential part of what it means to succeed. We face a new world and with it a new way to win. Many are being called – not all will be chosen.

Geert Hofstede, emeritus professor at Maastricht University, who studies cultural differences between countries, emphasizes that comfort with ambiguity isn't purely an individual trait. According to Hofstede,[8] countries with a high comfort with ambiguity have a high tolerance for opinions that are different to their own, dislike rules and are, overall, more contemplative.

According to Hofstede, Greece and Portugal are examples of countries with low comfort with ambiguity. Denmark and Sweden, by comparison, are high "accepting cultures" (high comfort with ambiguity).

In thinking about those who struggle with ambiguity, I am reminded of a story I have always enjoyed. At the height of the "Troubles," a tourist from Boston travelled to Ireland to visit the land of his forefathers. Towards the end of his trip, at the end of a long and tiring day he decided to stop in at a local pub. Well, he was having a fine relaxing time, minding his

---

8   The Uncertainty Avoidance Index is one of five dimensions of cultural differences that Hofstede uses. The others are power distance, individualism, masculinity, and long-term orientation. G. Hofstede, *Culture's Consequences* (Sage, 2001).

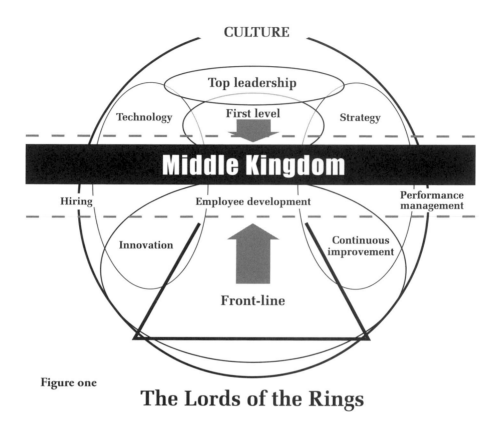

Figure one

The Lords of the Rings

own business and drinking a glass of Guinness when, out of nowhere, a tough looking fellow stuck a gun in his ear and asked him, "Catholic or Protestant?" Recognizing the dilemma he was in, the tourist quickly looked around the pub for clues. Not seeing any, but being a Harvard man, quick as a flash, he answered "atheist." Well, that threw the gunman for a couple of seconds, but then, with even more *gravitas* than before, the gunman demanded, "Would it be a Catholic or a Protestant God you don't believe in?"

Returning to that happy band who can play the game without goalposts, I also recall an experience early in my career. At the time, I was part of a small team responsible for industrial relations involving a workforce of 13,000 or so in the auto sector. British labour relations were at an all-time low. Being part of the bargaining team was, thus, a somewhat testy experience. At one bargaining session, with the room full of union reps, one of my colleagues caught the national official in what was clearly a carefully crafted "untruth." When this was pointed out, without batting an eye, the official leaned back in his chair, smiled broadly, and in a deep melodious Welsh accent, sang out, "Boyo, my philosophy in life is that if you can't ride two horses, you shouldn't be in the circus."[9] This is not to suggest, of course, that comfort with ambiguity has anything to do with duplicity.

Re-engaging the Middle Kingdom

Although what it means to be the "linchpin" has clearly changed and continues to change, it would be a mistake to write the middle manager's obituary anytime soon. As one era passes, another beckons. Don't worry if you can't find a black tie; in truth, it's a case of "the King is dead – long live the King!" Naturally, for King read Queen.

There is a strong case to be made that middle managers are potentially more important and, when provided with the tools, can have a greater impact than at anytime past. Everything – simply everything – goes through them. Indeed, more than ever, they are the Lords of the Rings. (See Figure one.)

The organization, be it a classical hierarchy, process-focused or virtual, still pivots around a relatively small number of people in the middle who bridge strategy with action; who bring the vision to life; who manifest, through the force of their own behaviour, the organization's values and, in doing so, help shape the culture. They are the people who iron out problems associated with the latest technology and who, when opportunity knocks, play a central role in making innovation more than a slogan.

It would be a mistake to write the middle manager's obituary anytime soon.

A cadre of management who link the top two tiers of leadership with the front line, who hire and grow tomorrow's talent, and who are uniquely positioned to respond to everyday performance problems make an undeniable contribution that isn't going to go away. Moreover, the less useful control via the rule book and the more important self-reliance and initiative become, the greater the potential influence of those who inhabit the Middle Kingdom.

Unfortunately, "should" and "could" are a far cry from "does." When asked about the contribution they make, middle managers don't talk about their "wins," personal job satisfaction, or even the growth curve they are on. What is top of mind, the emotional hairball that they want to cough up, is that, above all else, they feel overwhelmed, overworked, and,

---

9   "If you can't ride two horses at once, you shouldn't be in the circus" is attributed to James Maxton, a British Independent Labour Party MP from 1932 to 1946.

perhaps most damaging of all, overlooked. What all this means is that if organizations are to navigate complexity, make agility a way of life, and nurture innovation – as they must – literally nothing (nothing!) is more important than re-engaging the Middle Kingdom.

Moving forward clearly demands a new mindset regarding the role of those in the middle. Listening, really listening to what they have to say is no less essential. The core, the guts, the fundamental nature of the challenge, however, is getting middle managers back in the game.

Ten tactics for re-engagement

The following suggestions are far from complete, but the ten approaches outlined here are a really good place to start retooling the potential influence and contribution of your middle managers:

1. **Stop referring to "leadership" and "management" as if they exist in a different space and time.**

    Welcome to a mindset that has damaged the cause of the Middle Kingdom possibly more than any other. It's a mental model that starts from the assumption that leaders and managers are entirely different animals.

    The discussion goes like this: Leaders orchestrate change and managers implement. Leaders do the right things and managers do things right. Leaders set direction and managers budget, organize, and control. Leadership is about the quality of thought, and management is about attention to detail and follow-through – or some variation thereof. Julian Birkinshaw, professor of strategic and international management at the London Business School, puts it this way: "By dichotomising the work of executives (leadership vs. management), Kotter, Bennis and others squeezed out the essence of what managers do and basically left them with the 'boring' work that 'leaders' don't want."[10]

    The implications are writ large: Those at the top of the organization lead and those in the middle ... well, they **only** manage. It's a way to frame expectations that builds an organizational class system that, by inference, represents a not-so-subtle put-down of all of those who inhabit those oh-so-critical bridging roles in the middle of the business. And guess what! The underlying assumption is simply not true.

---

10   "Management: An experiment in reinvention," *People Management*, 16 July 2010, p. 23.

If those at the top of the business can't manage,[11] there is simply no way they will be able to implement strategy. And if middle managers don't know how to lead, they'll get stuck the first time they come across a new problem or opportunity. *You can't "manage change." You have to lead the way through change.*

This is not to suggest that top leaders and those in the middle of the organization have the same focus. Marcus Buckingham and Curt Coffman in their book *First, Break All the Rules*[12] advocate that the difference between the top and the middle of the organization is that the higher one goes, the greater the need to look outward. The late organizational psychologist Elliott Jaques was always quick to point out that each level of organization hierarchy demands a progressively greater ability to see into the future ("time-span of discretion").

Pride is a powerful ally and resentment an even tougher opponent. If middle managers are conditioned **not** to think of themselves as leaders, it's naive in the extreme to expect them to act like leaders.

> *Pride is a powerful ally and resentment an even tougher opponent.*

Action

> In all that you do and say, reinforce that **leaders manage** and **managers lead.**

> Make those in the middle feel that they are the solution and not the problem. Make them emotionally part of the future. Hook them into the big picture. Start by involving them, to the extent possible, in the business strategy. Make sure middle managers understand the thinking behind the strategy.

> Make middle management a key constituency in shaping the organization's cultural journey. No matter what those at the top mandate, if they don't buy in, little will change. Middle managers also represent an invaluable asset when it comes to defining (measuring): (1) today's culture and (2) the culture we need around here moving forward. In that, in all probability, they helped create it, those at the top of the house aren't always the most objective observers of today's culture. Those in the middle can afford no such luxury – they wrestle with reality every single day.

---

11 This was an early and enduring criticism of President Obama.

12 (Simon & Schuster, 1999), p. 63.

2. **Address change anxiety or accept that being an also-ran is the best your business can aspire to.**

There is a difference between holding down a job and fulfilling a role. In the former, the work drives what gets done and when. Those in a role have an opportunity to shape the nature of their contribution. A job is measured against a set of standards that are the same for every job occupant. Success in a role is measured against agreed-upon goals (ideally, a scorecard) tailored to the experience and capability of the individual. The end product being that the higher in the organization you are, the greater discretion you have as to how to use your time.

Today's middle managers have neither a job nor a role. Performance expectations come together in what might best be defined as a combination of job and role (JOB-role). JOB is presented in upper-case because in recent years more and more time is spent fixing problems (call it "**J**umpstarting **O**perational **B**reakdowns) – and less thinking about how to avoid those same problems. Middle managers are wrestling so many alligators that draining the swamp becomes impossible. If you could give the typical middle manager one wish, it would be that the emphasis move to the second four letters (ROLE) – **R**ealising **O**rganizational **L**eadership **E**xpectations.

Middle managers are so caught up in the day-to-day, so overwhelmed by the unending stream of problems that a new and destructive malady has emerged: change anxiety, or *changxiety*. The last thing in the world middle managers want to talk about is change. They know at a cognitive level it's impossible to ignore. They also know that change comes down to one simple, overriding issue – more work. If you're already working 60 hours a week and your family asks, "Who is that tired and weary stranger who appears at the dinner table every now and then?" dealing with one more change initiative ranks right up there with being asked to chew razor blades.

What we are describing is deeper and more problematic than simply pushing back against doing things differently. What is implied is a constant level of anxiety that makes the mere act of coming to work a Sisyphus-like burden.[13] If changxiety is part of your own organization's landscape, then expect (1) absenteeism/attrition from those in the middle of the organization to start to look like a flood, and (2) applications for middle management openings to become little more than a trickle.

---

13 As a punishment from the Gods for his trickery, Sisyphus was compelled to roll a huge rock up a steep hill – but before he could reach the top of the hill, the rock would always roll back down again, forcing him to continually begin anew.

Action

❭ Switch the prime organizational focus from customer satisfaction to the quality of work life of those who hold down positions in the middle of the organization. It may sound like business sacrilege, but if middle managers aren't happy, the chance that the customer will be well served is an illusion. The same is true of employee engagement generally.[14]

❭ Recognize that any and all organizations can successfully deliver only one truly major change initiative at a time. Stretch, engage, simplify, but don't overwhelm. When the pipeline gets jammed, nothing flows.

❭ Have managers one-level-up from middle managers start each day by preparing two lists. The first: what they can do to make the people who work for them more successful. The second: what they are personally going to stop doing. Encourage middle managers to embrace the same discipline.

❭ Find out how those in the middle of the organization really feel. Make these meetings face-to-face: focus groups, middle-management forums, breakfast sessions with a member of the top team – whatever it takes to get a handle on what middle managers are concerned about and what they need (not want) the organization to do about it. These meetings need to be anchored in humility and candour. Middle managers are reluctant to speak out. They figured out a long time ago that when you're neck deep in the nasty stuff and sinking, keeping your mouth shut is the smart thing to do. Don't call an audit of middle-management satisfaction an "engagement survey." Middle managers all too often see the engagement survey as (a) an opportunity for poor performing employees who have been on the receiving end of tough-minded feedback to get back at them, and (b) a vehicle that often breeds an ever-greater sense of employee entitlement.

❭ Balance what you can do for middle managers with a candid conversation describing what the organization needs (not wants) from them.

3. Re-establish a sense of pride in what it means to be a middle manager.

Consider the following: No matter how well thought through, your strategy is flawed. No matter how robust you think your point of commercial differentiation is,

---

14 In *First, Break All the Rules,* Buckingham and Coffman identify the employee's relationship with the first-line supervisor as the single most important factor in determining job satisfaction.

someone is out there, right now, figuring out how to do it better and faster. Whether you want it to be or not, your culture will be different tomorrow than it is today. And if you knew how many of your most talented people were in the job market right now, you wouldn't be able to sleep tonight.

Bob Dylan wakes up in the morning, looks in the mirror and says, "The times they are a-changin'". The only thing that can be taken for granted is that tomorrow will be different. The gate of opportunity swings both ways. When open, possibility beckons. When it's slammed shut, past practice represents the only way forward. And let there be no doubt, middle managers **are** the gatekeepers. Everything goes through them. They are the final arbiters of what is possible. Using an old adage, "If they are not for you, they are against you."

> *People don't resist change, they resist inadequate leadership.*

People don't resist change, they resist inadequate leadership. They resent being left on the sidelines. They balk at initiating a new way to operate when the outcome makes their life more difficult. They rail against that which appears to be unfair. They subtly derail the actions of leaders whose actions come across as self-serving. Middle managers want to be full partners in the change being enacted. They hate being told they have to change. They want to take pride in what they do.

Action

> Identify what those in the middle have to be proud of. Emphasize what makes the organization special. Make affirmation a way of life. Surface and share positive stories. Identify the early adapters and cameo their success. Catch people in the middle "doing it right."

> Encourage risk. Reward risk. Learn from what did not work. Celebrate glorious failures.

> Strip out all of the unnecessary bureaucracy – and there is, in all probability, a lot of it – from middle management work.

> Great organizations have a great (meta)story. Make that story live in the middle of the organization. Sweep away the sightlines between the work that middle managers do and how that contribution makes a difference in people's lives. Insist that regardless of the position, every middle manager spend time with a customer every month.

> Make the reason behind the change as important as the outcome needed. Ensure that the "here is why we have to act" conversation, even though the overall audience may be large, is eye-to-eye. Building trust is poorly served by trickle-down communication, webcasts, or video conferencing.

> Part company with any leader one-level-up who doesn't make developing those who work for him/her a compulsion.

> Insist that every key leader is mentoring two or three young middle managers from outside the leader's area of responsibility.

> Make terms such as "caring," "humility," and "transparency" central to how leadership success at every level is defined (e.g., a criterion for succession).

> Don't promote anyone into a key leadership role unless they are a great coach. Transfer to the competition anyone who isn't open to be coached. Yes, anyone, and do it soon!

4. Don't confuse downsizing with "dumbsizing."

In tough times, senior management justifiably makes the decision to reduce the workforce. Middle managers are then charged with carrying out that decision. Not necessarily with enthusiasm because, in doing so, they are metaphorically crafting a stick with which to beat themselves to death. "Success" means that not only will the middle manager have to work a good deal harder but, as the messenger who conveys the bad news, critical, often long-held relationships will have to be reworked anew.

The problem is exacerbated in that organizations take swaths of employees out of the business without fully thinking through how problematic this makes life for those who have to work with what remains. Beefing up skills in delegation, expanding decision-making opportunities, simplifying processes and/or changing the reward system to reflect the additional burden are all pushed to one side because keeping the ship afloat simply swamps even the best of intentions.

In talking to supervisors who work in customer-facing elements of the business, my own experience is that, time after time, I am told they get home after a full and often stressful day's work and are faced with two hours plus of business e-mails. They are trapped by "the juggler syndrome." Drop one ball and the audience (the manager-one-level-up) labels them a failure! Energy, enthusiasm and, for that matter, family life all suffer. It's an ongoing and, in many organizations, a steadily worsening malaise that permeates the attitude, vitality, and loyalty of the one group that shapes morale across the organization. Meanwhile, make no mistake: If you lose the goodwill of middle managers, then strategy is just another word.

Action

› Ensure that middle managers don't first hear about intended corporate actions in the media.

› Make sure that downsizing is accompanied by aggressive interventions aimed at simplifying key processes. Dropping marginal business lines, outsourcing and revisiting the number of offerings available are no less important.

› Go to the lengths necessary to make sure middle managers fully understand the background to, and the thinking behind, downsizing decisions.

› To the end possible, enact the downsizing in one single action. Dribbling it out, having people across the organization waiting for the next shoe to drop zaps the vitality of even the most resilient employees.

› Recognize the role middle managers play in downsizing and how emotionally stressful it is for everyone involved. Explore (non-financial) ways to recognize the effort that middle managers put in (e.g., days added to the next statutory holiday).

› Provide training and guidance to middle managers in how to manage the separation discussion.

› Expose middle managers to the content, quality, and value of post-employment support (e.g., outplacement).

5. **Make your middle managers feel special: Start with work–life balance.**

Coercive tension, anxiety, and a constant sense of being overwhelmed inevitably lead to one question: "Who is to blame?" And the group that middle managers put squarely in their sights are those at the top of the organization. It is a level of antipathy inflamed by ongoing scuttlebutt with regards to the executive golf membership, top-management retreats, business-class travel for short-haul journeys or any of the other benefits that have become commonplace for top management. To the points identified add over-the horizon salaries,[15] inflated termination payments, and the "you still win big if you fail" mentality that has permeated boardrooms in recent years.

There is more. Organizations talk about work–life balance; they run courses on work–life balance; they even make it a question on surveys, but enter into a discussion with today's middle manager about actually achieving any sense of work–life balance, and the likelihood is the response will be couched in the sort of language your grandmother warned you about. Many middle managers are further from work–life balance than they have ever been.

Meanwhile, because they have greater discretion over both their focus and time, senior managers are starting to recognize, and in many instances adjust, their patterns of work to reflect the need to have a full life. This in no way suggests that the latter isn't appropriate. On the other hand, if you see highly-paid executives leaving at a decent time, and you still have three hours of work to get through, it tends to work against you being a happy camper. Keep in mind, resentment is a form of behavioural virus – once it infects, whole programs become inoperable – and especially the one called "commitment."

> *Coercive tension, anxiety, and a constant sense of being overwhelmed inevitably lead to one question: "Who is to blame?"*

Action

> If middle management in your organization is dominated, or about to be dominated, by Generation Y employees, and work–life balance isn't part of the deal, think again. Of course, tomorrow's workforce demographics and the fact that the war-for-talent is back on means you really have no choice.

> If the organization is introducing new laptops, phones, etc., make sure those in the middle get them first. It's surprising how much prestige can be associated with simple actions.

> Have a middle-management website. Trends, dates, events, a classified section, who is moving up, job openings, technology tips, local entertainment – all make the site worth visiting.

---

15 People in the middle of the organization cannot conceive of the contribution demanded to earn the multi-million compensation packages that are becoming commonplace for those at the top.

> Make your middle management website "cool." Recognize that the social network generation finds anything that looks like a traditional presentation BORING.

> A middle management blog is a must. Consider also the benefits of an on-line, middle management magazine with lots of photographs, competitions with prizes for the kids, free trips, etc.

> Have your most talented middle managers complete a diary for six weeks. Reward those involved for doing so. The diary should capture the challenges that came up and what each manager did about them. Use that knowledge as the basis for better defining the middle management role – as well as selection, coaching, and ongoing development.

> Keep middle managers informed. Never allow a situation where the union rep knows first or is better informed. For union rep read "informal leader." Build communication tools/portals that make middle managers the first to know. Always! Effectively, cultivating the grapevine means that when people hear disquieting rumours, the person they go to, with confidence, is their own manager. In the enduring words of Captain Jean-Luc Picard[16] – "Make it so!"

6. Revisit how you spend your training dollars.

It's very easy to follow trends, to get trapped by the fashion of the day. Nowhere is this more true than in leadership development. What new program out there seems to have The Buzz? What leading-edge thinker, were we to bring them in, would bring heightened cachet to our overall approach? What new technology would make the next conference "exciting?"

Middle management training is particularly susceptible to the latest fad; overly influenced by the best-selling book by a well-known author; developed in the belief that what is good for those at the top of the organization makes perfect sense for those in the middle; prone to include learning activities that offer little more than high entertainment value. This is not to decry the potential value of ropes programs, training with horses, drumming, white-water rafting, etc. Indeed, if delivered as "learning as play"[17] (rarely the case) rather than "play as learning" (the norm), experiential learning can be an invaluable way to bring the learning experience to life.

---

16 Fictional *Star Trek* character.

17 It's important to distinguish between learning as play, and play as learning. The former shapes the activity such that it not only energizes the workshop but is designed specifically to drive the learning outcomes and culture the organization is seeking to create. Play as learning relies largely on the entertainment value of the activity – replicating a highly lauded activity from elsewhere, regardless of the overall outcome and development needs of the immediate audience.

Turning middle management training over to "the experts" isn't necessarily a good idea, either. Brilliantly led, interesting and stimulating though they may be, workshops focusing on business policy, blue ocean strategy, international marketing, quantitative techniques, and all of the other mini-MBA offerings – represent a poor investment. If you're drowning, being taught how to build a boat isn't very useful. You want to learn how to swim. You want to know **what** you can do differently on Monday morning – and **how** to do it.

Action

> Review all of your middle management training. If the bridge between content and "do differently on Monday morning" isn't clear, revisit the underlying assumptions.

> Make "hands-on" an anthem in **all** middle management workshop design. The following topics rank high on the middle management needs index:

- The hiring process[18]
- Employee development
- Performance management
- The tough conversation
- Listening
- Taking the team to the next level
- Using technology to enhance collaboration
- Employee retention
- Managing a multigenerational workforce
- Building a climate of affirmation
- Exercising greater influence
- How to inspire front-line employees
- Cultivating "the grapevine"
- Storytelling
- Mentoring

---

18 The reality is that, regardless of their role in the organization, few leaders know how to hire talent in today's business environment. What makes this difficult to explain is that the hire decision may well be the most single important decision any leader makes.

- Asking great questions
- Management-of-self

⟩ Listen to the customer. Identify what the customer's unmet needs are. Involve middle managers in both defining and in structuring the training focus. Ensure that the design aligns content, stories, language, metaphors, and the speed of action implied with the culture the organization is seeking to create.

⟩ Identify pockets of middle management excellence and find ways to have those involved share that experience across the organization.

⟩ Know that 80% of all development takes place on the job. Understand that training middle managers, but then not training the manager one-level-up in the same skills, is to negate much of the potential value of middle management training.

⟩ Find out who the very best middle managers are and make them part-time trainers and workshop leaders. It is great recognition for them personally and unlocks value in a way that no one from outside the organization can.

⟩ Select a small cadre of outstanding middle managers who are close to retirement and make them full-time mentors. Not only does this give them a unique opportunity to leave a legacy, but it will mean that the invaluable knowledge and insight they have won't walk out the door when they do.

⟩ Websites and other learning portals are an invaluable resource. However, not everyone takes to on-line learning. To leverage this investment, ensure that workshops are supported by easy-to-access, Web-based training material. Make sure that when people need to act on-the-job, what they learned in the workshop is brought to life again on-line.

⟩ Find creative ways to measure in what ways middle management training makes a difference.

No organization has only one culture. With that in mind, all leadership development and training, regardless of the level, should emphasize what might best be called "leadership reach." By "reach" is meant an ability to read the context and act accordingly be the culture, in question, strongly hierarchical, allowing significant discretion to act, or allowing almost unlimited freedom along the lines of "skunkworks."[19] Throw

---

19 Created by Lockheed, "skunkworks" describes time, space, and resources set aside where teams are given almost unlimited freedom to act (play). For some teams, in companies like Google, this can amount to 30% of their time. Needless to say, innovation flourishes in these hothouse cultures.

different suppliers, customers, and countries into the mix, and what leaders are capable of getting their arms around becomes a make-or-break issue.

7. Push for mastery in hiring.

One of the most disruptive trends in recent times has been the notion of folding not just the support needed, but the final hiring decision into a shared services model. Use expertise, access to training and development, guidance, and evaluation by all means, but when middle managers no longer make the final hire decision, an essential connection (premise for loyalty) has been lost.

There is a strong case to be made for **expert support** (the key word here being "expert") to middle managers in the hiring process. In *Outliers,*[20] Malcolm Gladwell emphasizes that mastery demands 10,000 hours of practice. Only someone involved in talent acquisition all day, every day could even come close to investing the requisite 10,000 hours needed for true mastery. But support is not the same as making the final decision.

Fortunately, in the majority of organizations, middle managers still decide who they want on their team. Indeed, if one looks across virtually any organization, middle managers control the talent pipeline. The central problem being that the hiring tools they work with – developed largely by and for the boomer generation – are often misaligned with the challenge at hand. Examples include: looking in the same old places for the same old people; rudimentary training in interviewing, compounded by the inadequacy of behavioural interviewing techniques that simply don't work with today's candidates;[21] little support for defining and evaluating "team fit"; literature and website support for recruitment that fails to factor in the highly developed visual literacy of people under 35. And no less damaging – a sink-or-swim approach to bringing new people on board.

They may have stubbed their toe over the accelerator issue,[22] but Toyota is an awesome competitor. Before they make the hire decision, they INVEST thirty-two hours in the recruitment of every front-line employee.

---

20 (Little, Brown and Company, 2008), pp. 35–68.

21 Designed by "boomers," it worked well for a generation that moved between organizations infrequently. Today's candidates are not only seasoned interviewees, but in many instances, better trained in how to answer behavioural questions than the interviewer is in how to ask them.

22 As of January 2010, Toyota had announced recalls of about 9 million vehicles worldwide for a "sticking accelerator pedal" and floor mat design problem.

Is front-line recruitment a strategic investment in your organization, or is it, as in the case with many businesses, a hurried, hit-or-miss process that gets in the way of doing the real work?

If hiring **by** middle managers is important, think how vital the hiring and promotion **of** middle managers is. The qualities displayed by a great teacher are quite different from the competencies needed to be a successful school principal. Promotion based on technical capability is equally problematic. Tom Peters, in his book *The Little Big Things: 163 Ways to Pursue Excellence*,[23] suggests that for any "boss selection process" organizations should give as much attention to the promotion decision as they give for an acquisition. Few organizations come close to that standard.

And the middle management qualities organizations should be looking for? In his *Harvard Business Review* article "In Praise of Middle Managers,"[24] Quy Nguyen Huy suggests a successful middle manager is all of the following:

> ❯ Entrepreneur: quick to see problems, works from the big picture, has diverse work experience, generates rich ideas.

> ❯ Communicator: strong credibility, plugged into broad and deep social networks, sells change, can fire up people in non-threatening ways, knows how to get things done.

> ❯ Therapist: keeps anxious employees productive by addressing emotional needs, provides one-on-one problem solving and support.

> ❯ Tightrope artist: balances change with needed continuity, "keeps the company working."

Although there is clearly a danger in assuming that every middle management position is, more or less, the same, Huy's suggested middle management qualities provide a provocative framework. Not least is the fact that he describes ways to operate that would be extremely difficult to identify in the traditional interview process.

In that times move on, to the characteristics identified by Huy in 2001, today, one would want to add:

- A strong sense of self
- Speed of action

---

23 (HarperCollins, 2010), p. 272.

24 September 2001.

- A winning mindset

- Comfort with ambiguity

- Cultural reach

- An ability to work successfully with different generational groups

- Intellectually nimble

- A quick learner

- Tough-minded

- Resilience

- Technology savvy

- Ability to build and lead strong teams

- All of the qualities that come together to make a great coach

Action

> Stop promoting people based on their technical ability. Start promoting people based on their managerial potential. If you do the former, you will certainly lose an invaluable operator and may well have to live with a mediocre supervisor.

> Recognize that every hire decision is a million-dollar investment. Train managers accordingly – especially those who do the most hiring. Build a best-in-class hiring process. Don't allow anyone, especially those in pivotal roles, to shortcut the process. If you operate internationally, know that the hiring process has to reflect cultural, legal, demographic, and social differences.

> Make diversity a way of life. If the overall mix of those on the team doesn't reflect the diversity of those the team serves, there is work to be done. Diversity isn't just about people per se. Edward de Bono, inventor of "lateral thinking," suggests that how people work (e.g., patterns of work dominated by routine) inhibits innovation. He urges organizations to bring creativity to everything they do, from the shape of the glasses employees drink out of to how teams make decisions.[25]

---

25   Michael Costello, "Innovation: The thoughts that count," *People Management,* 29 July 2010, p. 29.

> If you are not investing as much time, effort and money in middle management selection/promotion as you do on buying an expensive piece of equipment, revisit your priorities.

> Talent acquisition is built on four pillars of fit: (1) leadership fit, (2) performance fit, (3) team fit, and (4) culture fit. When one pillar is weak or missing, the whole structure is unsound. (For more on the hiring process, see Chapter five.)

> Make the individual responsible for the organization-wide hiring process one of the most talented, seasoned and yes, highly paid executives you have. Don't under-hire for this role. Don't make this a developmental position. And, don't, under any circumstances, delegate critical aspects of the hiring process to your purchasing department. The illusion of saving money today can have a profound impact on long-term organization success. Would you ask a plumber to rewire your house?

> You can't hire the best middle managers unless you attract the best. Build a great story. Get that story out there. Do it every day, in every way. Be creative. (For more on the building blocks of a great story, see Chapter three.)

> Build an environment where everyone in a leadership role strives to hire people who have the potential to be better than he/she is.

> Cast a wide net. Use every avenue known to man (and, of course, woman) to source middle management candidates. The range and added-value of on-line recruitment tools is growing exponentially. Take advantage of them all!

> Hire strategically.

> Invest time in why middle managers stay with the organization. Feed that insight into the hire decision.

> Track hiring success. Don't make the mistake of promoting those who have a questionable track record in hiring.

> Refresh people's hiring and recruitment skills regularly – **at all levels.** No excuses – those who suggest they don't need to attend the workshop being offered are invariably the ones who need to be there the most. Even if they are recognized experts, they should be there to share that expertise. And remember, as society changes, so does the need to retool the talent acquisition process.

> Use an external consultant to debrief recent middle management hires. Make continuous improvement in hiring a leadership mindset.

8. Push for mastery in employee development.

When the game changes, it changes for everyone. Because legendary baseball pitcher Cy (Cyclone) Young had such a dominant fastball, in 1892, the National League was forced to move the distance from the pitcher's mound to home plate from 50 feet 6 inches to 60 feet, 6 inches. And yes, a good many of the established pitchers fell by the wayside. During the 1968 season, Bob Gibson, the St. Louis Cardinals right-handed pitcher, another hall-of-famer, registered a 1.12 ERA.[26] His strikeouts-to-innings ratio approached 1.0 and, at one point, he won fifteen games in a row. In response, Major League Baseball lowered the height of the pitching mound from 15 inches to 10 inches for the 1969 season. Change is a given. The ability to grow in response to that change is not.

Your organization has a cadre of people, any of whom could rightly be called "Chief Talent Officer." The reason: The enthusiasm (or lack thereof) of those in the middle of the organization bring to developing members of their team has a huge (HUGE) influence on results, retention and the day-to-day effectiveness of the business.

The problem: Middle managers discover that growing and developing talent brings more problems than plaudits; they learn that downplaying the talent on their team is the smart thing to do.

Here is how one supervisor put it to me: "I go to great lengths to hire great people … I put my heart and soul into coaching, stretching, testing, and developing those same individuals … key players on my team flourish … they become targets for roles elsewhere in the organization … I regularly lose key people … I get little or no recognition for adding to the organization's talent pool … I am constantly working with green talent … I get criticised if I don't meet/exceed targets … I have to put in extra hours to make sure the job gets done … *I get the message.*"

Action

> Reward those in the middle for developing talent.

> Give middle managers the tools they need to grow talent.

> Insist (insist!) that every supervisor, manager, and executive identify and develop a successor.

---

26   Earned run average: the average number of runs given up per nine innings.

9.   Push for mastery in performance management.

Organizations become great for different reasons. For one business, it is the nature and speed of innovation (3M). For another, it is the ability to remain the lowest-cost provider (Walmart). For a third organization, it could well be the flair and excitement they bring to launching and marketing their products (Apple).

> *Regardless of the source of their competitive advantage, organizations that endure have one thing in common: the discipline of delivery.*

Regardless of the source of their competitive advantage, organizations that endure have one thing in common: the discipline of delivery. What we are describing is an unrelenting focus on results – both short- and long-term; an inner strength around getting things done that never wavers; a habit-based response to each and every challenge; a programmed instruction that is never overwritten by the contingencies of the day. And who propagates and delivers this discipline? Middle management! Clear goals, ongoing dialogue, affirmation, coaching, feedback, timing, and, where demanded, the tough conversation make for strong middle managers.

Strong managers make for strong teams. Strong teams build a strong culture. And your culture is the **only** element of competitive advantage that is sustainable.

Top management regularly emphasizes the need to build a "results-driven culture." What they are really saying is, "We need those in middle management roles to bring the discipline of delivery to **everything** they do."

Action

❯ Insist on the discipline of delivery from the top down (i.e., leaders at the top of the house must be seen to be accountable).

❯ Have a "broken windows" philosophy[27] – that is to say, the discipline of delivery starts with the everyday things: meetings start and end on time, health and safety issues are religiously adhered to, absenteeism is addressed early in the cycle.

❯ Build a performance management process that gives equal weight to the agreed results (what) and organization's espoused values (how). Confront and separate,

---

27   Based on a sociological theory by James Q. Wilson and George L. Kelling that early action to fix problems like broken windows in the inner city will prevent further vandalism and crime. Mayor Giuliani put the theory to the test in New York City with his policy of "zero tolerance."

if necessary, those who don't live the organization's values, regardless of the results being achieved.

> Don't delegate – even a modicum – of the organization's performance culture to anyone other than those who hold a managerial role. Don't allow past practice, a history of conflict, or an especially difficult union representative to soften that resolve. Back middle management such that poor performance carries appropriate, timely, and consistent consequences.

10. Make middle managers part of the solution.

People respond to challenge, to opportunity, to an invitation to rework the processes that dictate how things get done. With the best of intentions, if new ways to be are parachuted in without fully taking into account the opinions and concerns of those impacted, conflict can be assumed.

Action:

> Even if it's not working all the time and only occurs in small pockets of the organization, what's working? How can you build on that? What role can middle managers play in bringing about the needed change? Explore ways in which that energy can be released.

> Technology offers a host of new ways for middle managers to collaborate. Sharing best practice, peer-to-peer coaching, seasoned middle managers mentoring those new to the role, knowledge building, providing positive feedback and generally taking advantage of today's networking tools – all these enable middle managers to play a pivotal and active role in co-creating their future contribution.

> Something as easy to use and inexpensive as Skype[TM][28] can transform the ongoing relationship between middle managers working for the same company but operating out of different plants or offices. Candour, respect, and trust all change when you put a face to the voice. Self-organizing communities of interest have the potential to bring down barriers, enhance efficiency, improve decision making, simplify processes, strip out waste, increase the speed at which things get done, and stimulate innovation. To wit: Collaborative networks provide a unique opportunity to get middle managers back in the game. *Don't let the competition do it first!*

---

28 Skype™ is free video/audio conferencing software with a peak of 23 million users online as of 2010. Recent advances in handheld devices enable video conferencing to take place anywhere, anytime.

Imagine a truly world-class soccer team. The forward line is drawn from South America's most talented players. In that it is made up of Europe's finest, the defence is no less impressive. The basis of an unbeatable team, one might think. Except, as any good coach knows, the game is won or lost in the middle of the field. It is decided not by those who make the headlines because of their scoring prowess, but by the craft, creativity, and commitment of those – often unheralded players – who link defence with attack.

The modern organization is no different. A great strategy counts for little if it is not implemented. A great product is merely an offering in a box if it's not supported by an agile and committed team. The role of the middle manager is changing. Knowledge and authority are no longer enshrined in the same body. Speed of action demands greater freedom of decision making for those who interface with the customer. Multiple teams, the networked organization, and ever-changing patterns of collaboration have diluted the supervisor's formal power whilst, at the same time, emphasizing the need to get things done through influence.

None of the above means that the era of middle management has passed. Middle managers are still the most important employees any organization has. Everything still goes through them. They are still the Lords of the Rings.

No team can win if their mid-field is watching the game from the sidelines. No business can thrive if those who inhabit the Middle Kingdom are discontented, disillusioned, or discouraged. And no organization can ignore the reality that when middle managers no longer care, front-line employees no longer dare!

Unleashing the potential of middle managers would result in:

_____

_____

_____

_____

_____

_____

_____

_____

As an organization, to get middle managers back in the game, we must:

_____

_____

_____

_____

_____

_____

_____

_____

Starting now, to ensure that the talent in the middle of the organization is better utilized, I personally commit to:

_____

_____

_____

_____

_____

_____

_____

_____

Chapter two:
NOW, MORE THAN EVER, CULTIVATE THE GRAPEVINE

In an upside-down world

Re-engaging the Middle Kingdom means understanding the role played by the informal organization. It means, in particular, "managing" the influence and impact of the informal communication channels. In the recent past, the grapevine was viewed as a fact of life – a competitive force that shaped opinion but, assuming the formal communication processes were orchestrated with professionalism, one that could be kept in check. That was before the social networking revolution took off. That was before the aggrieved, the cynical, the hard done by, were given access to an electronic pulpit. That was before those who felt that, to serve the greater good, their opinions simply had to be heard were gifted a plethora of communication tools that put an already super-fast grapevine on steroids.

The narrative of the trapped mind

"Gossip goes on. We would like to stop it; we try to stop it, but every effort we make seems to create even more gossip."

"Social networking sites like Twitter are a constant source of frustration – especially when a specific manager is being criticized, castigated, or ridiculed. The dilemma is that it's a self-fulfilling force that's all but impossible to control."

"I can accept that the generation now joining the organization has a different view of the world. But isn't pampering them just a great way to reinforce the "it's all about me" mentality that many of them already bring to the job?"

"Our job is getting the product out and responding to customer concerns. The rest – what people say behind my back – well, I'll let someone else worry about that."

The rest of the story …

Manage the grapevine or it will manage you!

Now, more than ever, cultivate the grapevine

"Cyber-gossip, for that's what much of today's social networking sites are really all about, amounts to little more than traditional forms of gossip on steroids."

Man is a naturally curious creature. When threat or perceived danger enter the picture, however, that in-born curiosity is quickly replaced by a compelling "need to know." When faced with what we don't know, we examine what we do know, look for signals or symbolic acts that suggest what is actually happening, talk to our peers, factor in past experience, and then simply make the rest up. As a species we are really, really good at making stuff up!

Welcome to the most perfect communication system known to man! "Perfect" may be something of an exaggeration, but don't underestimate the effectiveness of the grapevine. There are no upfront costs. No one needs to approve "the message." It is unhindered by policies, procedures, or the corporate agenda. Formal structures and guidelines are skirted with ease. International boundaries are as if irrelevant. It is truly dynamic; it can move in any and all directions at the same time. As for speed of delivery, only the Internet can compete, and even there, cyber-gossip and social chatter fills much of the bandwidth.

As if that were not enough, the research suggests the grapevine in the modern organization is up to 80% accurate. If it were packaged as "networking software," it would be a killer application. By comparison, corporate communication teams have access to little more than a bow and arrow when compared to the sophisticated weaponry those in the informal organization have at their fingertips.

The term "grapevine" came into common usage during the American Civil War. The tangle of telephone wires that followed the army, many strung haphazardly from trees, were said to look like grapevines. The often confusing and garbled messages these lines delivered led Union soldiers to refer to "the grapevine telegraph" as a way to describe gossip and unreliable rumours.

The term may have become popular in the nineteenth century, but story, rumour, gossip and, in times of crisis, a need to know represent a form of human expression that had already reached full flower before lining up to look at the latest cave paintings become *de rigueur* on a first date. Or, as zoologist Robin Dunbar[29] puts it, "Gossip is to humans what grooming is to our ape cousins." Chimps, incidentally, spend 20% of their day on grooming.[30]

Feeding the grapevine

In addition to the obvious – sickness, drought, hunger, and the perils of the hunt – our evolutionary experience was fashioned by two fears: (a) the unknown visitor and (b) being rejected by the tribe. Our survival has thus honed within us an extraordinary ability to (1) read the landscape, (2) quickly recognize and share information that suggests danger, (3) be highly attuned to actions that might cause one to be cast aside by the community, and (4) constantly assess shifts in power and status. Because we now work in factories and offices doesn't mean that those survival characteristics have been lost. Those early experiences still define who we are – they still inform how we interpret the world around us.

(1) **Gathering information.** What keeps people awake at night isn't so much the prospect of being "outsourced"[31] as it is not knowing what the future holds. The grapevine serves to fill that gap. By pooling knowledge, employees are working to strip away uncertainty. By floating different scenarios, they are tapping into what might be described as the organization's collective wisdom. By testing their own assumptions about the future, they are seeking to reduce the possibility of personal failure. When uncertainty rules, the grapevine thrives!

> *When uncertainty rules, the grapevine thrives!*

Grapevine advice: Recognize that what you don't say is often more important than what you do say. Don't make promises you might not be able to keep.

(2) **Gesture.** Those at the top of the organization live in a goldfish bowl; the higher in the organization, the greater the magnification. When concern and doubt enter the equation, that magnification is increased several-fold. When an optimistic and cheerful leader starts to wear a frown, the organization notices. When the CEO walks onto the elevator and forgets to say hello, things must be about to get worse. When meetings are cancelled without warning, people look to take cover. Some gestures (like the unprecedented visit of a senior HR executive from head office) carry such symbolic importance that they scream "Danger!" Whether deeply symbolic or

---

29 Robin Dunbar is an anthropologist at Oxford University.

30 Richard Conniff, *The Ape in the Corner Office* (Crown, 2005), p. 145.

31 Outsourcing is now impacting virtually every sector of the economy. India, for example, has a million lawyers and graduates 200,000 new lawyers each year. Not only are the standards very high, but their legal system is very similar to our own. A lawyer in India earns $25.00 an hour.

not, unfamiliar or disquieting signals are merely harbingers of tomorrow morning's "best guess." The dilemma: What people make up, if not corrected, sooner rather than later, becomes not just the perceived truth, but in many people's eyes – the only truth.

Grapevine advice: Not knowing is always far more damaging to morale than a harsh and difficult-to-accept truth. People can deal with what they know. What fuels heightened anxiety, what employees don't forgive is when their (highly developed) read of the landscape suggests danger, but those they need to trust remain silent.

(3) **Gossip.** Every now and then, a business writer will talk about "purging the organization of gossip." Good luck on that! Gossip is an inborn and indelible part of our make-up. It's locked into our DNA. We gossip for a number of reasons. Gossip, literally, makes us feel good.[32] Gossip gives us status: Being "in the know" carries with it the aura of importance. Gossip expands and strengthens our social network. Gossip enables us to validate the organization's values. Forget what the plaque in reception says, the organization's real values are all about who succeeds and who doesn't; what behaviour is rewarded and what actions draw censure. Utilizing the corporate version of the garden fence, gossip also allows employees to "test" what actions are deemed acceptable to their peers.

> *Those who shape the language control how people see possibility.*

There are two sets of rules: (a) the rule book and (b) the rules as defined by the informal organization. The level of productivity, the number of suggestions coming forth, support for change initiatives, what it means to be a member of a successful team, and the degree of candour all owe far more to the "informal rules" than anything management can impose. Gossip disseminates, subtly explains, and validates what those informal rules are. Here one needs to keep in mind that censure exercised by the informal organization is far more effective than any disciplinary procedure. Meanwhile, a juicy rumour is nothing more than gossip tied with a big red bow.

Grapevine advice: Those who shape the language control how people see possibility. Language rooted in the past, metaphors that play on people's fears, unhelpful satire,[33] and stories that focus on the negative all pass power to those within the informal

---

32 Mutual grooming by primates stimulates endorphins, which, in turn, reduce heart rate and other signs of stress.

33 The power of satirical humour: There is no doubt that, during the 2008 US election, comedian Tina Fey's depiction of Republican vice-presidential candidate Sarah Palin on *Saturday Night Live* in the "I can see Russia from my house" sketch did her political aspirations a great deal of harm.

organization who would prefer things to stay the way they are. Create/instigate/ share the metaphors and stories that describe tomorrow's success. Don't make the mistake of allowing the language that dominates to be introduced by employees (creativity is not a function of role in the hierarchy) who may not share the goals and aspirations needed for the business to succeed.

(4) **Game playing and the silent grapevine.** Sit in on any marginal team and you quickly discover that loyalty and drive have been replaced by game playing. Many of these "games" are tried and true, such as "the real problem lies with ..." [fill in as appropriate: government regulations, corporate, marketing, the customer, the software, etc.]. Other games, such as defensive tactics that hold the team back from engaging in truly candid conversations, are often created by, and are unique to, the team. Unique or not, the games played cannot continue without tacit support from those on the team – especially the team leader. That support comes not from anything spoken, but from nuance and signals that combine to communicate a self-regulating message delivered on a silent grapevine.

In the best of times, the games played provide a self-fulfilling comfort zone that allows team members to avoid both personal risk and collaborative actions that demand trust. In the worst of times, those same games provide impenetrable walls and barriers that people will be only too quick to hide behind. Inappropriate messaging conveyed and reinforced through game playing feeds and then continues to feed the silent grapevine.

Grapevine advice: Surface and then confront those who either orchestrate or hide behind "the game." Make candour a way of life.

(5) **Getting even.** Whenever an individual feels they have been treated disrespectfully or unfairly, several options lie open: to buckle down and get on with things as if nothing had happened; to confront the individual in question; to seek redress by complaining to the manager of the person concerned; or to get even. In that it involves the least risk, the latter option is often the most appealing. Getting even means subtly pulling back support. It means being less than forthcoming in sharing information. And if the person whose behaviour has caused offence happens to be the team leader, getting even means using the grapevine to resourcefully sow seeds of doubt about their capability. Damaging enough when one person on the team

uses the grapevine this way, when several members act in concert, the team leader's reputation can be damaged beyond repair.

Grapevine advice: Treat people with respect. If that doesn't seem to work, treat people with respect. And as a last resort, treat people with respect!

Cultivating the grapevine

Jon Katzenbach, founding partner of a New York City-based consulting firm, in talking about the informal organization, suggests that successful managers "must understand the constellation of collaborations, relationships, and networks, particularly in times of stress and transition. We're not saying you can formalize the informal," says Katzenbach. "We're saying you can influence it more than you do."[34]

To understand the power and elegance of the social networks inside your organization one need look no further than what movie buffs call "the Kevin Bacon effect." According to one source, there have been 150,000 motion pictures made featuring 300,000 or so named members of the cast.[35] The Bacon number (BN) is the shortest route between any of these individual actors and Kevin Bacon, a film actor with a prolific screen career. A BN of 1 is someone who appeared in a film with Bacon. A BN of 2 is a film actor who appeared in a movie with someone who acted in a movie with Bacon. What is remarkable is that the vast majority of those 300,000 actors have a Bacon number (BN) of 3 or less.[36] Extrapolate that insight to your own organization and you get some idea of how truly wired the organization is; how elegant its social network is; and how quickly and easily information (rumour) can, and does, flow. As an aside, the Kevin Bacon phenomenon goes a long way to explain why "word-of-mouth marketing" is so impactful.[37]

Considered by many managers as an unwarranted hindrance, the grapevine is an inescapable fact of organizational life. Leaders who ignore it take a huge risk. Leaders who seek to suppress it are destined to be frustrated. Leaders who seek to manipulate it are likely to be strangled by it. The grapevine is real, it shapes behaviour in a profound way, and lack of attention merely makes it stronger. We have to recognize the power and influence of the grapevine; we have to bring it out from the dark hallways and shaded corners and expose it to the harsh light of truth. Like the successful vintner, we have to understand that if we let it grow in an uncontrolled fashion, its product will leave a sour and bitter taste. On the

---

34 *Fortune*, July 2007.

35 Philip Ball, *Critical Mass* (Farrar, Straus and Giroux, 2004), p. 353.

36 See http://www.cs.virginia.edu/oracle/ to see how this works.

37 This concept of human interconnections is also known as the "six degrees of separation" – the theory that a person can be connected to any other person in the world through a chain of only five acquaintances.

other hand, if we learn to work with it, if we know how to cultivate it – it can sustain us. What follows are ten ways to cultivate the grapevine, ten actions that you can take, starting on Monday:

1. **Tell people the truth.** For most of the 1930s, the majority of Europe's leaders including British prime minister Neville Chamberlain either ignored, misrepresented, or sanitized the truth surrounding German rearmament. Winston Churchill's parliamentary response: "Tell the truth to the British people; they are a tough people, a robust people .... If you have told them exactly what is going on you have ensured yourself against complaints and reproaches that are not very pleasant when they come home tomorrow on some disillusionment."[38] People know when they are hearing only part of the truth, the truth slanted to meet the needs of the speaker, language that lacks a sense of fairness, and/or anything that smacks of manipulation. Don't hold back. Share the numbers. Be honest about future sales. Let people know what's really going on. Or as Churchill puts it so powerfully, when you withhold the truth (today) you are sowing the seeds of tomorrow's disillusionment.

2. **Be optimistic.** Telling people the truth doesn't mean the message has to be stripped of hope. To do so is to create a vacuum of uncertainty that invites the malcontents of every stripe to fill the void. Because our interpersonal antennae are programmed to look for external threat, unduly pessimistic scenarios have the potential to be both contagious and self-fulfilling.

> *We have to recognize the power and influence of the grapevine; we have to bring it out from the dark hallways and shaded corners and expose it to the harsh light of truth.*

Optimism, meanwhile, has to be based not just on the possibility of future success, but that those at the helm truly believe in a brighter tomorrow. This belief has to be present in both the language used and, equally important, the signals those at the top send out. The posture, the tone, the sense of confidence behind the message is, in many senses, "the real message."[39] That is not to say the language itself isn't important. Words like "downsizing" suck the energy out of any business. "Positioning the

---

38 William Manchester, *The Last Lion* (Little, Brown and Co., 1983), p. 683. Churchill's comment was made in 1932.

39 Drawn from Marshall McLuhan's writing on the theme of "The Medium Is the Message."

business for future success" conveys the impression that today's sacrifice has a purpose. Remember, people imitate and take on board the emotions of those they trust and admire.[40]

3. **Get into the middle of the organization.** The modern wonders of communication clearly have their value. At times of crisis or disruption, however, people want that communication to be personal. They want to look top leaders in the eye and make their own judgement about whether they are hearing "the truth." This means "town hall" meetings, breakfast sessions, standing on a box on the shop floor, or any other communication process that allows openness and integrity to shine through. And while on the topic of getting buy-in during difficult times, don't allow key meetings of your team to conclude simply with what has been decided. To do so is to invite everyone at that meeting to convey their own version of the decision made. Agree on specifically what everyone in the room is going to say – even if that means committing "the message" to paper.

4. **Seek out the informal leaders.** Leadership has little to do with what it says on the business card. Leadership is defined by the people we choose to lead us. Many of the organization's most influential leaders don't appear on the organization chart at all. Yet despite that, they make a difference; they influence opinion, and when times are tough, they are often the ones people turn to. These informal leaders can provide insight into how people really feel, how the communication from the top is being received, and where confusion still exists. And where trust and respect has already been established, these same informal leaders can be the means whereby ill-formed gossip is confronted and/or positive messages grafted onto the grapevine. As Gareth Morgan points out in *Images of Organization*,[41] "Alliances and coalitions are not necessarily built around an identity of interests; rather, the requirement for these forms of informal organization is that there be a basis for some form of mutual beneficial exchange." Always keep in mind: One influential, informal leader can steer the mood of an entire group.

5. **Recognize that Gen Ys and their younger cousins are different.** Take a look at your corporate website. The probability is that it was commissioned for an audience who grew up with newspapers. Those in your organization who are age thirty or

---

40 It is believed that so-called mirror neurons drive us to subconsciously "ape" the behaviour of those we interact with. This need to fit into "the community" is a programmed survival response.

41 (Sage, 1997), p. 173.

less don't read newspapers, they lack the attention span[42] to go through a document that isn't succinct, and they ignore anything that looks like their dad might have written it. Blogs, Facebook, Twitter, text-messaging, and their interactive, real-time cousins have, for this generation, all replaced yesterday's traditional forms of communication. Or have they? The technology is new. The underlying emotional needs being satisfied, perhaps not so.

Cyber-gossip – for that's what much of today's social networking sites are really all about – amounts to little more than traditional forms of gossip on steroids.[43] It is nevertheless a communication channel you cannot ignore. As with more established forms of gossip, you cannot allow it to run rampant. And as with the rest of the grapevine, you must cultivate the Web-based and social networking channels. If you don't yet have a small team whose role in life is to work the cyber-grapevine, then pull one together as soon as you can. And, don't forget, winning the loyalty and respect of your Gen Y generation today is an important investment – that is, if you want to have a business a decade from now.

6. **Put the supervisor back into the equation.** The one thing that damages organization spirit quicker than anything else is when the supervisor appears to be ill-informed. When the supervisor doesn't know, if employees read about it in the newspaper first, where there is a communication vacuum the union can exploit, or where the latest scuttlebutt, in whatever form, becomes the primary information source, those at the sharp end of the business quickly form an opinion that management doesn't have an interest in their wellbeing. Train supervisors in how to hold regular briefing groups. Train those same supervisors in how to deliver those "communication briefs."[44] Make sure that the information contained is up-to-date. Have the supervisor invite questions from their team. Anticipate as many of those questions as possible when the brief is prepared. Make sure the supervisor is given a response to the questions they couldn't answer at the meeting, such that they can get back to the employee within 24 hours.

Finally, if you operate across international boundaries or have a multicultural workforce, make sure that the team who prepares the supervisory briefs is sensitive to the needs of different audiences. As for managing the grapevine, never forget that

---

42 A number of neurologists are firmly convinced that the Internet is reducing people's ability to concentrate. See "Is Google Making Us Stupid?" *The Atlantic,* August 2008.

43 Anthropologists such as the previously quoted Robin Dunbar suggest the maximum number of people with whom we can build stable social relationships is no more than 150. Interestingly enough, this approximates the size of a village before humans walked out of Africa.

44 A "communication brief'" is a specially prepared communication package presented by those in supervisory roles, to the extent possible, across the organization at the same time.

the most important communication asset you have are the men and women who sit right in the centre of the organization – your middle managers. Don't leave them on the sidelines.

7. **Make storytelling a key leadership competency.** Organizations are full of stories. The dilemma: When times are tough, the negative stories get additional airtime. Negative stories hold people back. When negative stories abound, even the most agile organization puts on heavy boots. And make no mistake, you can't get rid of those negative stories by trying to get rid of negative stories. You merely create yet one more negative story.[45]

The way forward: Make the stories you tell so compelling, so vibrant, and so vivid that they strangle the negative stories to death. Bring positive stories to meetings which emphasize your organization's story;[46] which provide examples of breakthrough thinking; which display success in the face of adversity; and which celebrate your most recent heroines and heroes. Remember, negative stories can inform, but only positive stories inspire. If your stories don't dominate the airwaves, someone else's will! The best stories allow people to see their current reality through a new lens. If your leaders don't excel in storytelling, enact that training now.

8. **Put energy into the "engagement process."** Know that there is a distinct relationship between climate and how the vine grows. The simple rubric here is that when people feel engaged, they feel that their opinion matters. For example, when employees are given the opportunity to rework the processes that define how things get done, instead of complaining that they don't know what's going on – they do what any self-confident and proactive person would do: They ask!

This assumes an engagement process is more than an annual paper-and-pencil exercise. It takes for granted that each team has an opportunity to address the issues that come up in the survey. It presumes that team members are given the freedom to act and that stretch, personal growth, and ongoing development are woven into the very fabric of the organization. It speaks to a culture where challenging the way things are is a way of life. It also means, of course, that those at the top listen to the suggestions made and then act.

---

45 For more on storytelling, see my book *Leaders Must Lead!* (Executive Forum, 2003).

46 In that culture is story and story is culture, your organization's story is a rich and multi-faceted picture of either the culture you have or, depending how the story is framed, the culture you need to create.

Employees who believe they have a future with the organization have a vested interest in challenging the negative aspects of the grapevine. When they are unsure or confused, committed employees take the trouble to find out what the truth is.

Fear makes the grapevine stronger. Unnecessary rules make it stronger. Unwarranted formality makes it stronger. Lack of transparency makes it stronger. Revisit the organization's approach to engagement. Don't get trapped into defining success based exclusively on what "top 50" list you are part of. The real question is, "Are your people engaged by the work they do?" As a rule of thumb, the greater the alignment between how people would choose to work and how they actually work, the more the grapevine starts to become an asset rather than a handicap.

9. **Amplify the organization's values.**[47] Successful organizations live their values. In turbulent times, they go to the extra trouble of making those values central to everything the organization does. Stories, symbolic acts, how leaders respond to crisis represents the "soil" from which the grapevine – positive or negative – takes nourishment. When leadership behaviour amplifies those values, negative rumours find it difficult to put down roots. When employees know (really know) what the organization stands for, then inappropriate gossip has little to feed on. And when caring, consistency, and respect are a way of organizational life, then those who habitually prefer to see the glass half full are robbed of an audience. There is a reason why great organizations like Four Seasons attract and retain the best.

10. **It's not enough to lead – you have to inspire.**[48] Power moves into a vacuum. Not sometimes, not occasionally and not just "when the time is right." Power always moves into a leadership vacuum. When disquiet, personal worry, and doubt about the organization's direction enter the picture, the grapevine becomes the informal organization's safety blanket. When those with formal authority are hesitant, lacking in commitment, or appear to be driven by self-interest, the grapevine will work to fill the void. When leaders are inconsistent or deal with people in a way that comes across as being unfair, the grapevine is strengthened. When leaders hold back the truth, the grapevine replaces "not knowing" with a heightened level of speculation.

Leaders inspire when they personally display a passion for the journey being charted, when they show an unswerving determination to go the course. People need their

---

47 Guiding principles.

48 For more on inspirational leadership and the power of the grapevine, see my book *Myth, Magic, Mindset: A Template for Organizational Culture Change* (Executive Forum, 2008).

immediate leader to be a role model. They need the leader to bring a sense of purpose to the team. They need the leader to always put the needs of the team first. Inspirational leaders agree on stretch goals, recognize and fan the flame of each team member's unique capability, give people the opportunity to show what they can do, build a climate of affirmation and then celebrate success.

People are inspired when they learn from each other. Leaders who inspire embrace the unconventional. They know when and how to let their imagination out to play. They see diversity not as individual difference but as a means to access different perspectives and, in doing so, better understand what lies around the next curve.

> *Every time an employee talks to, or serves a customer, it is inevitable that the messages carried on your grapevine bleed into that conversation.*

Leaders who inspire work to keep their feet on the ground. The best Roman commanders employed a slave whose primary role was to regularly remind his master that, despite past victories, he (the master) was merely mortal.[49] Knowing that delivering on any and every promise, caring, and a willingness to listen, are what ultimately make people trust them, leaders who build followership need no such reminder. The most effective response to a grapevine that is running wild is inspirational leadership. In times like these, people want to be inspired, they need to be inspired, and when they are, today's concerns start to look a whole lot like tomorrow's opportunities.

Two-thirds of all customer defections have little to do with price, technology, or the product. Customers vote with their feet, for the most part, as an outcome of how they are treated. Every time an employee talks to, or serves a customer, it is inevitable that the messages carried on your grapevine bleed into that conversation. Failing to cultivate the grapevine means, by implication, you are not managing the customer experience and nothing, literally nothing, is more important to your business.

Predating written history by tens of thousands of years, the grapevine thrives because it serves a meaningful purpose for our kind. Because it's about a common cause wrapped in symbolic human interaction, it also, much of the time, makes us feel good. You can figuratively take a

---

49 In *Rome Triumphant: How the Empire Celebrated Its Victories* [1962] (Barnes & Noble, 1993), Robert Payne writes, "it was the anonymous slave standing behind the triumphator, whispering in his ear about the vanity of honours, who represents the greater triumph" (p. 251).

flame thrower to it, pour weed killer on it or try to tear it out by its roots – one thing remains certain: **It isn't going to go away.** Ignore it and it will grow stronger! On the other hand, work with it, cultivate it and understand how to reap its rich harvest, and the grapevine can become an invaluable cultural asset.

Where lies the future? The 2010 Soccer World Cup in South Africa had, as does any international competition, its high points and its lows. Amongst the lows were international stars who didn't shine, referees who couldn't see, the unheard-of World Cup phenomenon of empty seats, and a ball that, literally, flew. On the lowest rung of dissatisfaction, however, was the vuvuzela, a horn-like instrument that the locals blew vigorously and constantly throughout every game.

Of cultural interest for the first two minutes, it quickly became apparent that the cacophony of meaningless noise being produced totally destroyed the atmosphere of the game. Gone were the singing, the chants, and the music of the bands the teams brought with them. Missing was any contribution the fans could make in encouraging their own team. Lost even was the samba drum beat that traditionally accompanies every Brazilian team. In its place, a constant and wholly distracting blast that (literally) filled the airwaves with what sounded like a swarm of angry African bees waging war with a competing hive. Even the players on the pitch complained that they couldn't communicate with each other.

There is a metaphor here for tomorrow's cultural challenge. Taking into account the emerging technology, the unprecedented access employees have to public space, and the masterful skills younger people possess in social networking, when it comes to the potential that lies with informal communication processes, we ain't seen nothin' yet. Indeed, employees haven't even started to explore the many ways in which they can "blow their own trumpet."

Cultivate the grapevine today, or – take it as a given – it **will** strangle you tomorrow! If it isn't cultivated, if it is allowed to run wild, the grapevine will overwhelm your organization with a level of self-serving noise that, vuvuzela-like, will drown out your story. If you sit back and simply hope for the best, then the beat of your samba drums, the positive stories, the shouts of encouragement, and everything else that reinforces what it is that makes you special will be overwhelmed by the incessant, wholly distracting, angry-sounding buzz of the crowd.

As an organization, were we to cultivate the grapevine, we would benefit in the following ways:

_____

_____

_____

_____

_____

_____

Working harder to nurture the grapevine means that, as an organization, we have to:

_____

_____

_____

_____

_____

_____

Starting now, to better influence the grapevine, I will:

_____

_____

_____

_____

_____

_____

Chapter three:
IF YOU'RE NOT MANAGING YOUR CULTURE, SOMEONE ELSE IS!

In an upside-down world

Be it re-engaging middle managers, supporting rapid growth, instilling organization agility, or building a business that attracts and retains the best, at the end of the day, it's all about culture. Yesterday, leadership drew on our need for certainty. A reliance on business strategy, for example, draws on the assumption that the future will unfold in a way that has a degree of predictability. Today's leadership has to embrace "not knowing." With uncertainty comes the reality that what guides possibility, what has primacy, what endures, what will be around after the strategy has been rewritten – is the organization's culture.

The narrative of the trapped mind

"We don't have time to focus on something as vague and esoteric as culture."

"If you can't measure it, you can't address it."

"We're just a small group involved in a business start-up. Culture is something we'll clearly have to take a look at – but not until we're much bigger."

"Culture is the prerogative of the top team. In my role, I can only hope they communicate effectively what I need to do differently."

"We address culture through the work we do around engagement."

"We can't really work on culture because we don't have one culture – we have many."

"Human Resources are working on it."

The rest of the story …

Your culture will change whether you want it to or not.

If you're not managing your culture, someone else is!

"The expression 'change the culture' is a misnomer. If elements of what you need tomorrow don't exist today, it is virtually impossible to create them."

Nature offers lessons to us all. When the wind blows strongest, it is the tree with the capability to bend that survives. Growth based on yesterday's success, rigidity, strength without agility, may well be acceptable when the sun is shining and the wind is calm, but in the midst of a gale, not being "change-ready" can bring down the sturdiest oak.

We are living in turbulent times. Faced with uncertainty, leaders have the choice: (1) to complain, (2) to capitulate, (3) to contemplate, (4) to compromise, or (5) to bring about change. Change, of course, means taking people with you. Not so easy when many of those who fill front-line roles are suffering from change burnout. Not so easy when the organization's culture is viewed as a mysterious and impenetrable cloud.

When the tempest rages, those who survive and grow are not the most aggressive, the toughest, or even the smartest. Evolution teaches us that survival lies largely in the capacity to adapt. Put a different way, your ability to ride out the next storm rests on the extent to which your organization has made culture an integral part of the leadership conversation.

Think about the following questions: (1) On a scale of 1–10, how important is culture to your organization? Almost without exception, managers, regardless of level, tend to answer "9" or "10." (2) Now think about the amount of time your team invests in strategy, budgeting, business planning, and other work aimed at creating tomorrow today. Using the same scale, attribute a "10" to that bundle of activities. By comparison, also on a 1–10 scale, think about how much time **your** team commits to shaping tomorrow's culture. When we pose that question to the same group of managers, the answer is typically a "2" or a "3." The dilemma: Leaders of all stripes recognize the importance of culture but don't spend much, if any, meaningful time on it.

"Cultural drift" – doing little about it but at the same time assuming that somehow, magically, your organization's culture will end up where you need it to be – is naivety writ large. Sadly, it's where 90% of today's organizations (public and private) dwell.[50]

---

50   As reflected by our own research.

By way of stark contrast, Herb Kelleher, the founder of Southwest Airlines said, "Culture is one of the most precious things a company has, so you must work harder at it than anything else."[51] Southwest Airlines is the world's most successful airline, posting a profit for the 37th consecutive year in January 2010. Isadore Sharp, the founder and long time Chairman and CEO of Four Seasons wrote, "In looking back over the past forty years, I've identified the four strategic decisions that formed the foundation of Four Seasons. They are known as the four pillars of our business model. They are quality, service, culture and brand."[52] It's tough to argue with the philosophy of an organization that is, simply, the best.

When was the last time your team had a truly transformative conversation about organizational culture? In what ways was the most recent hire decision assessed in terms of the culture you need to create?[53] What are you doing to regularly measure your organization's culture – "Where are we and where do we need to be?"[54] If your answers amount to "not recently" or "very little," then your culture is managing you. Does it matter? In an upside-down world it matters a great deal.

What follows are thoughts and questions that frame the culture conversation.[55] An initial response might well be along the lines that it is something we intend to get to. There's a story about Napoleon that offers an interesting point of view about timing. When told by one of his marshals that the French had lost the day, he looked up and said, "That may be so, but there is still enough time to make sure we win tomorrow's battle." And for all of us there will be a new battle in the morning!

> *When was the last time your team had a truly transformative conversation about organizational culture?*

The culture conversation

Why does culture get short-changed? For some teams, culture is too abstract, too vague, too difficult to really get to. Other groups recognize the importance of culture but it remains an issue on their "to do" list. The biggest barrier, however, is more basic – even top teams simply don't know how to have the culture conversation.

Culture isn't an abstract, will-o'-the-wisp sort of thing. It's real, it lives, and how organizations shape their culture has a profound impact on an organization's ability to thrive and survive.

---

51 Kevin and Jackie Freiburg, *Nuts: Southwest Airlines' Crazy Recipe for Business and Personal Success* (Broadway Books, 1998), p. 144.

52 Isadore Sharp, *Four Seasons: The Story of a Business Philosophy* (Penguin, 2009), intro.

53 This implies that your search provider brings, as needed, culture measurement tools to the table.

54 John O. Burdett, *Without Breaking Stride: Successfully Moving into a New Role* (Executive Forum, 2009).

55 John O. Burdett, *Myth, Magic, Mindset: A Template for Organizational Culture Change* (Executive Forum, 2008).

Viewed all too often as an HR project, when uncertainty becomes the norm[56] the need for the organization's culture to be a top team imperative emerges with full force. The conversation around culture, regardless of where or at what level in the business it takes place, benefits from the following insights:

> Rule number one: If you're not managing your culture, someone else is – the competition, the unions, a key supplier, leaders seeking to carry out their own agenda, influential members of the informal organization.

> Rule number two: Never forget rule number one.[57]

> Part of the human condition is the need for a sense of belonging. The untapped power of culture is that it not only builds community (mutual support in pursuit of a common cause) but is a place where people can feel they belong. A strong culture is by far the most effective way to attract and retain talent.

> Leaders live in a goldfish bowl – the higher in the organization the role, the greater the magnification. Misalignment between what the organization is seeking to become and how top leaders behave is a sure-fire way to put a brake on even the best thought-through culture initiative.

> Any meaningful work around culture should keep in mind that culture isn't an end in itself. The culture we need around here must support that which, going forward, we need to achieve. It's ultimately about business performance. To that end, shareholder expectations, tomorrow's customer needs, the emerging political reality, the competitive climate, demographics, and the talent pool within the organization must inform any and all conversations around culture.

> No business is an island; the organization's culture will reflect the changing face of society – whether you want it to or not.

> Culture exists at different levels. On the surface are those indicators that are easy to identify such as dress, language, overt behaviour. The deeper one goes, the more defused become the signals about what is really going on. When one touches bottom, there lie issues such as mindset, identity, and ingrained values. The golden thread that links the myriad parts (of culture) that make up the whole is a blend of technology and learning. To ignore or overlook either in any conversation around

---

56 For "uncertainty" read "new entrants to the market," "aggressive growth," "acquisition, "turnaround," and/or "economic disorder" generally.

57 Rule number one/rule number two is usually attributed to Warren Buffet.

culture is the equivalent of building a wall without considering the quality of cement needed.

❯ Where strategy and culture collide, culture wins – every time. In an unstable world, culture trumps strategy. In turbulent times, your culture will be around long after the agreed strategy has been through the shredder. Where the only thing we can say about strategy with confidence is that it will change, thinking based on the presumption that strategy **drives** culture is, of pragmatic necessity, being replaced by the reality that the culture **enables** strategy. When you next meet to agree the strategy, if culture isn't afforded the same attention, you are, figuratively, building a house of straw.

❯ A leader who says, "We are going to change the culture around here" has stumbled at the first hurdle. The underlying message to those listening – "you are the problem" – is a criticism that everyone in the audience will resent. With resentment comes resistance. "Shaping" the culture, moving the culture in a new direction is a far more accurate and respectful form of language. Here one needs to add that if the executive at the front of the room actually believes you can blow up today's culture and in the near future create something **totally** new, the suspicion he/she is prone to random and unexplainable flights of fancy needs to be taken into account!

> *A leader who says, "We are going to change the culture around here" has stumbled at the first hurdle.*

❯ The expression "change the culture" is also a misnomer. If elements of what you need tomorrow don't exist today – not necessarily everywhere or all the time – it is virtually impossible to create them.

❯ Culture isn't about everyone being the same. Culture is a container for diversity. Too much diversity equals chaos. Too little, and nothing changes.

❯ Few, if any, organizations have only one culture. The challenge becomes to encourage diversity at a local level while, at the same time, build a strong overarching corporate culture. Being **both** tight and loose – knowing what is truly sacrosanct (e.g., the common purpose, shared values, leadership competencies)[58] – is where

---

58 For coaching, hiring, or talent management purposes, generic, organization-wide leadership competencies should be complemented by competencies that are role-specific.

judgment, wisdom, intuition, mental toughness, and a feel for connectivity enter the leadership equation.

> Leadership is no longer about "leadership style." It's about "styles." Like a great pitcher facing a new batter, it's all about the ability to adjust. It's about being adaptable enough – without losing one's true self – to work in different ways with different parts of the organization. For "different parts of the organization" read "different leaders," "different customers," "different countries," "different levels of value creation," "different degrees of risk."

> Even the most determined and aggressive leader cannot reconfigure the culture through fear, threat, edict, or censure. How does it happen? To take people forward demands trust, transparency, and timing. Those who work in and for the organization **are** the culture. It's the constituency that chooses who to follow. In doing so, they ultimately determine what is possible. Employees don't come to work to hold back who they are or what they can contribute. They do, however, withdraw support from a leader they don't believe in.

> In any organization, there are two dominant, often conflicting, forces. A way to operate as described by the organization chart – and the way things really happen.[59] The only day of the week when the formal structure dominates the informal is one that does not have a "y" in it.[60] Managing the informal organization is all about servant leadership. When the way forward rings of self-interest; when leaders decide both the what and **the how**; and/or when those who are impacted by the change aren't afforded the opportunity to play a role in orchestrating that change – then more of the same is the best outcome possible.

> Inviting those who are impacted to be full partners in the journey shouldn't lead to the tyranny of consensus. There are a number of key decisions impacting culture (e.g., mission, values, leadership competencies, structure, and technology) that can, and should, only be taken at the top of the house.

> The most important (two) groups in any organization are (1) those often referred to as "middle managers" and (2) anyone who interfaces on a day-to-day basis with the customer/client. The first are, literally, the only people in the organization who

---

59 Culture is found in the conversation that takes place when the boss leaves the room. It's what the men and women on the loading bay believe is important.

60 The "only day of the week" language comes from a comment Warren Buffet made about shares he didn't want to buy.

can bring about change. The second are the only ones in the organization who can build sustainable success. Impacting the culture means top leaders must look those who populate these powerful influence groups directly in the eye and explain with total integrity **why** the culture has to move in a new direction.

› Although a focus on both is essential, climate should not be confused with culture. The former is how people feel about the organization (employee satisfaction) on any one day. The latter is what **causes** them to feel that way. One is software. The other is the operating system. Climate is the flower of the lily floating on the surface on the pond. Culture is symbolized by the roots anchored firmly in the mud at the bottom of the pond. Invaluable as, for example, the ubiquitous engagement survey is, and although elements of culture are almost certainly captured, it should not be assumed that "engagement = culture." If issues such as symbolism, speed, structure, systems, storytelling, shared values, candour, brand, history, teamwork, language, metaphor, measurement, and mindset are not embraced by the engagement instrument, then a good deal of what is being described here as "culture" has been overlooked. That people are happy about the ship they are on doesn't mean it isn't about to hit an iceberg. Anyone remember the Titanic?

> "*Although a focus on both is essential, climate should not be confused with culture.*"

› You can't redefine the culture through a series of standalone actions. Culture is a system[61] and, as with any system, when you change one element you impact the whole. To that end, work on culture should not be confused with the body of work over the past two decades referred to as "change management." The difference is rooted in mindset and as such is significant. Change management speaks to the "burning platform," the notion of resistance to change,[62] and first remove obstacles. Change management seeks to first ask, "What's broken?" Culture is far more about shaping, adding to, and building on what's there. Change management is both mechanistic and incremental: break the problem down into its component parts and address one piece at a time. Culture is holistic: work the context. Change

---

61 That culture is a system doesn't mean to say that all of the elements have to be addressed at the same time. The challenge: To know what "thread" to pull first, while at the same time, to take into account how early initiatives influence the rest of the system.

62 The best way to build resistance to change is to run a program on resistance to change.

management is all about "alignment." Culture is best described by the term "harmony." [63]

> Without inspirational leadership little is possible. "Inspire" comes from the Latin *inspirare,* which means to breathe life into. To lead is to breathe life into the culture every single day. Yesterday's leaders emphasized the need to motivate. Today's leaders seek to inspire. The former is about trying to bring about change from the outside-in (extrinsic). The latter is about creating the conditions whereby the individual or team discovers the core of their own potential, from the inside-out (intrinsic). Inspiration shouldn't be confused with charisma. Inspiration drives us on; charisma draws us in.

> Culture is strongly impacted by the layout, colour (pink defuses aggression), degree of informality (encourages innovation), and overall design of the workspace. The use of common space (the organization's village green), the amount of light (stimulates learning), the feeling built into the design that the organization cares about its people (Google provides free food and "chill-out" places), the playfulness and nature of the furniture (round tables encourage collaboration), and the subtle signals contained in quirky little nooks and unconventional use of space – all carry an impossible-to-ignore message about what it's like to work around here.

> *Culture is story and story is culture.*

> Culture is story and story is culture. The organization's culture comes together and is manifest in the organization's (meta) story. Your story is your identity. Your story is the bedrock of your culture. If you have a great story to tell you had better tell it because no one else is going to. When all is said and done, it's not organizations that compete – it's stories. It's not the compensation and benefits that draw great talent to your organization – it's your story. A great story answers four fundamental questions:[64]

1. Where are we headed?

2. What do we believe in?

3. What make us special?

4. What is it we do that makes a difference in people's lives?

---

63 In Chapter four, this mindset shift is described as the difference between the mind of the watchmaker and the thinking of the potter.

64 To what extent does your organization's employment brand answer these four questions?

❯ Before talking about the building blocks of the culture conversation, a few cautionary comments to those charged with facilitating that conversation be they in Human Resources, part of a team that directs the strategic planning process, or working as an internal consultant:

- The simple exercise of describing "from what to what" (the culture we have and the culture we need) is often pushed to one side, ignored altogether, or overwhelmed by a cloud of mystique. Capturing the "what to what" (and why)[65] is a simple, compelling and essential first step.

- Organizations are far more comfortable working on the culture drivers (moves the culture forward) than they are on the culture anchors (holds the culture back). Key drivers include strategy, brand, process, structure, technology, the human resource systems and the espoused values. The cultural anchors include history, language, metaphor, myth, symbolism, storytelling, how people learn, and the ingrained values. To move the culture in a new direction is to work with equal endeavour on both the culture drivers and the anchors.

- When key leaders talk about **changing** the culture, that may not be what they really mean. More often than not, what they have in mind is to take the current culture to the next level. To that end, it is really important at the outset to scale the scope of culture change (1-10) being suggested. This is an exercise that is especially helpful when conducted with different groups or levels inside the organization; for example, the top team, middle management, the human resources team.

> *The top team doesn't always have an accurate read on today's culture.*

- The top team doesn't always have an accurate read on today's culture. Because they created it (or at least supported it) and because they often hear what others want them to hear, those at the top have a tendency to see the organization's culture through rose-coloured glasses.

- In describing (measuring) the emerging culture, two issues are of paramount importance. The first: Any discussion about the culture we need has to be

---

65   The **three Ws** of all, and any work on culture.

grounded in pragmatism. It's far too easy for the conversation to slip into what those around the table aspire to become. The second issue: "What's possible?" has to be complemented by "What's sustainable?" Factored into the latter is the sense of urgency needed to energize and continue to energize a new way to think and act.

Managing culture

First, don't forget rule number one: If you're not managing your culture, someone else is. Culture is a shared pattern of behaviour transmitted and expressed through symbolism, habit, and story. The dilemma: Culture is the sum of **many** parts. To manage culture thus means first surfacing, and then working on the **levers of culture change.** To that end, the culture conversation is brought to life through a number of key questions.

Here it is important to keep in mind that although those at the top of the organization have a unique responsibility for defining the emerging culture, "breathing life into the emerging culture" defines leadership success, regardless of level in the organization. Whether you are the CEO, a country manager, or run a small service team, the spirit and intent of the questions that follow have meaning for your team:

1. Do we have a compelling mission/purpose? Is the mission/purpose such that it makes people want to get out of bed in the morning?

2. Is the nature and degree of diversity[66] within the organization representative of those in the marketplace the organization serves?

3. Do we consistently live the brand **promise** inside the organization? Brand isn't just a promise to the customer, it's a commitment to every employee. If that promise doesn't live inside the organization, there is no way it can thrive in the marketplace. Here it is important to distinguish between the following:

    (a) The brand image is a simple, emotion-laden message that, through language, imagery, symbolism, and, on occasion, humour, connects the customer to the product or service. The brand image is all about getting the customer's attention. It's what initially differentiates one commodity from another. In the supermarket, it's what delivers point-of-sale emotional impact. The right brand image builds the first sale.

---

66   Diversity here is intended to embrace a much wider definition than is traditionally applied.

(b) The brand promise builds customer loyalty. Richard Branson and his PR flair (he is the master of getting people's attention) do much to project a cool and risk-oriented image of Virgin. His crazy acts may draw people to his airline, but if his flights are late, the toilets dirty, or there is even a hint that the pilots take risks, customers will not return. Consistently delivering on the brand promise in a timely manner is what brings the customer back.

Brand is one of the basic elements of marketing. At its core, its nucleus, the "glue" that makes the product or service "sticky," the "satisfaction factor" that defines the customer experience – is the organization's brand promise. The organization's culture needs to reflect, drive, and deliver that promise.

(c) In a market where there is little real difference between leading competitors, design can have a big impact on both the brand's image and the customer experience. Apple, for example, delivers a triple competitive threat: (1) It has an unbeatable brand image; (2) it delivers real clout in its brand promise; and (3) in Jonathan Ive's designs, it has a range of leading-edge products that many consider modern works of art. Add a truly inspirational leader, and one starts to understand what makes Apple so difficult to compete against; what makes its culture so special. For now, that is. [67]

4. Is it recognized that the speed at which things happen is a critical piece of the culture puzzle? Is it appreciated that when the speed is recalibrated by one competitor, it changes for all. Being the best counts for naught if you are about to become one of the slowest. In their HBR article,[68] Jocelyn Davis and Tom Atkinson suggest that business leaders need to differentiate between operational speed (moving quickly) and strategic speed (being on the right track). In a study of 343 businesses, they found that organizations with a "go, go, go" approach were far less successful than those that "slowed down to speed up." Simply put: When it comes to going faster, effectiveness trumps efficiency. Speed is one thing, time is another. You can measure speed, but time is an issue of perception. Until the fourteenth century, people's lives were governed by the changing seasons. There was little or no concept of a future beyond Mother Nature's clock. We've come a long way since then, but countries and organizations, for that matter, still differ in terms of their perception

---

67   Beyond the hype: In response to the iPhone 4 customer complaints, CEO Steve Jobs was forced to admit, "We're not perfect." You've got to believe that must have hurt!

68   "Need Speed? Slow Down," *Harvard Business Review*, May 2010.

of time – especially as it relates to a past vs. future orientation. The most dramatic example of this is the Taliban, whose raison d'être appears to be to recreate society as it was in the middle of the seventh century. For such groups there is no future, little concept of the now, only a belief that what was is what should be. Because of their history, buildings and artifacts, Europeans are, taken overall, more attached to the past than future-oriented. A 300-year-old building in Europe is relatively new. In North America it would be a tourist attraction. Add great weather to the equation, and it is easy to understand why California is the natural birthplace of organizations such as Apple, Disney, Oracle, Cisco, and Google.

5. Does the approach to strategy (e.g., a single strategy or a series of strategic scenarios) reflect the reality of the tumultuous times we live in? An effective strategy delivers focus. A great strategy develops alternatives.

6. In line with the culture we need to create, are we measuring and rewarding the right things? For example, does your organization's performance management system reinforce where and what you have been, or does it shape tomorrow's culture?[69] There is nothing new in the relationship between compensation and culture. In the period up to 1913, Ford had to hire 1,000 people to retain 100 workers. Henry Ford's answer was his famous "$5 dollars a day" minimum wage. That was over double the average wage of the day. Instead of a revolving door, Ford had men lining up for jobs. Ford also created new customers for his car. His remark at the time could be an anthem for the current age: "Purchasers are made, not born."

7. Does the talent management system work for us? Are we hiring and promoting the people in line with the culture we need to create? Does the leadership development agenda underscore the culture we need to create? Is the same true of coaching/mentoring conversations? Is cultural insight central to the organization's (post-hire) leadership integration process?

8. Is it understood that all change is rooted in language? To that end, is the need to listen, the value of storytelling, the power of metaphors, the impact of symbolism, and the act of letting go rooted in every team's consciousness? If you don't change the conversation, where you are is where you are destined to be.

---

69 Not addressing the performance management system **early on** is a common flaw of organizations that stumble when reworking the culture.

9. Do **all** of those in key roles live the organization's values? To "manage culture" is to have zero-tolerance for those who don't live the organization's values – no matter how successful they are in delivering results. In today's organization, the term "values" is a tricky concept. Ask a 50-year-old what is meant by the term "loyalty" and then ask a 25-year-old and you get a very different response. Overlay a multicultural dimension, and the degree of confusion is multiplied ten-fold. Arguably, organizations are not, nor should they be, in the personal values business. A far more meaningful term is "guiding principles." However, because it is the language in current use, the term "values" is used in the rest of this book.

10. Does the work on process improvement and reinvention seek to solve the problem of the day or is it aligned with who we need to become? To what extent is the latter true with regards to the technology we are about to introduce? In 1927, when Warner Brothers introduced sound into the movies *(The Jazz Singer),* not only did Warner's shares go from $9 to $132, but the industry was changed forever. When the technology changes, continuing to work on becoming better at what you have always done in the way you have always done it (e.g., making better silent movies) tends not to be the smart option.

11. Do we regularly revisit the organization's structure? When structure is on the agenda, are speed, simplicity, and span of control top of mind? Most organizations have too many levels. Remember, every unnecessary level doubles the noise and halves the effectiveness of the organization's formal communication processes. Too many levels also make the organization's informal communication processes (e.g., grapevine) far more effective than they would be otherwise.

12. When the bear in the corner growls, do people listen? Is candour alive and well generally? Is it alive and well on my own team? Do people say what is on their mind or does being open entail a degree of emotional risk that most people would rather avoid?

13. Do we have a winning market-facing value proposition (why buy from us)? The value proposition draws together all of the human, technical, organizational, and economic threads that deliver customer value. The brand promise is a simple way to express what that value is.

14. Do we have a winning employee-facing value proposition (why work here)? In the long run, having a winning employee-facing value proposition is more important than having a differentiated product or service.

15. Do we have a great story? Are we able to surface and share that story?

16. Do those who wear the mantle of leadership inspire others to follow them? Do those same individuals breathe life into the culture every single day? Is the spirit of affirmation part of the organization's DNA?

Who owns the culture? If culture is seen as something that the organization does to you or as the exclusive prerogative of those who drive a company car, not a lot is going to change. There were a good many reasons why the Roman Empire was around as long as it was. One of the prime reasons lay with a man of humble origins named Gaius Marius. A supremely gifted leader, he created what might justifiably be called "the first professional army." He standardized training, recruited commoners (before that a soldier had to own property worth 3500 sesterces in value), and equipped them at the expense of the state. His most sweeping change, however, was that the reward for serving with one of the legions for twenty years became the grant of land. He also initiated a policy whereby allies of Rome were awarded Roman citizenship. Being a soldier was no longer all about the threat of death on one hand and servitude on the other. The average soldier was no longer just part of the army – he **was** the army. He didn't just fight for Rome – he **was** Rome. Ownership changes everything. Julius Caesar learned a lot from his uncle Gaius. So can we.

Three colliding forces fashion today's economic and business reality. The first: the harsh reality of globalization and everything that implies (e.g., the rise of marketing and with it the dominance of the consumer). The second: advances in information technology (e.g., cloud computing, new avenues of mass collaboration, many-to-many communication systems) that open the door to, hitherto, untried organizational forms. Both of these "advances" have received wide business press coverage. A third factor has, however, gone largely without comment: cultural complacency.[70] As competitive intensity increases with low-wage areas of the world and recognizing, for example, that India will soon have more English speakers than

---

70 The evidence is that less than 30% of employees bring their 'A' game to work.

the US, facing a twenty-first century economy with a 1990s mindset around organization culture is the business equivalent of trying to hold off a hungry tiger armed only with a broken stick.

Your business future lies in having a better strategy, a far greater ability to innovate,[71] **and** a culture that is adaptable enough to dance around the razor-sharp claws of the competition. Simply put: Continued cultural drift sounds the death knell of your organization's economic prosperity. John Legend's song "If You're Out There"[72] has a line that could well be an anthem for all of us: *The future started yesterday and we're already late.*

And don't forget rule number one: if you're not managing your culture, someone else is. And rule number two is?

---

71 Canada has the poorest record of any country in the G7 when it comes to innovation.

72 From the Evolver album. GOOD Music and Columbia Records.

If we focused on culture more than we do, the organization would benefit in the following ways:

_____

_____

_____

_____

_____

As an organization, to better manage our culture, we must:

_____

_____

_____

_____

_____

Starting now, to ensure that my team isn't trapped by cultural drift, I will:

_____

_____

_____

_____

_____

Part two:
TAKING THE TEAM
TO THE
NEXT LEVEL

"Teamwork is the fuel that allows common people to attain uncommon results." – *Andrew Carnegie*

Chapter four:
YOU CAN'T CHANGE THE TEAM BY TRYING TO CHANGE THE TEAM

In an upside-down world

Yesterday, when the team struggled, the team leader's actions were invariably dominated by what can best be described as the mind of the watchmaker: *What (who) is broken that we need to fix?* In a world marked by talent shortages, today's team leaders seek to first rework the context. What they understand is that ideas, story, beliefs, meaning, and metaphor are the prime movers of change. What they practise is an approach to leadership that follows the way of the potter: "Work **with** the clay – not **on** the clay."

The narrative of the trapped mind

"Eventually, the challenges the team faces will work themselves out."

"When I stand back, it's clear that if we 'fix' a couple of people on the team, we'll really move ahead."

"Look, I know if you asked one or two members of the team, they'd suggest that as the leader, I'm part of the problem. I don't buy into that point of view."

"Fred is a problem from a team perspective, but he's a high performer personally."

"Teams aren't that difficult to understand. I'm thinking a robust 360° feedback session will probably fix what ails us."

The rest of the story …

The team is the basic building block of organizational life.

You can't change the team by trying to change the team

"Behaviour changes, not when we focus on the behaviour but when we build a new story, when we change the context, when we reframe the intrinsic motivation of those on the team."

You are on a number of different teams. On one, you may well be the team leader. On another team, you will be a team member. On other teams you will be a collaborator or an occasional team member. You are also likely to be leading teams or have teams reporting to you as part of a matrix structure where teams may be very different from each other. One thing is certain: Teamwork and your contribution to the teams you participate in are critical to your leadership success.

The team is the basic building block of organizational life. Mastery in working with, and leading teams is thus not an option. The challenge: How to get the best out of the talent around the table both as individuals and collectively.

We are team animals

Before the Industrial Revolution, an agrarian economy both emphasized and relied upon cooperation. It was the financial success of textile mills in harsh, smoke-filled North of England towns like Manchester, Blackburn, and Bolton that sent us down a track where the individual worker became the basic currency of commerce. And when the economists' love of specialization met the miracle of "Scientific Management" early in the last century, simple, standalone, mind-numbing jobs supported by increasingly complex processes became the only show in town. Community, collaboration, and the capability to self-organize came a bad second to short-term results, wasteful hierarchy, boss-ship, lack of trust, and the work study engineer's cheap stopwatch.

Because humans have brains that allow us to do things that the other primates cannot (storytelling, imagery, advanced language), we tend to forget that, as mammals, we are programmed to operate (and flourish) in groups. It was through teamwork, and all that the term implies, that we outlived more aggressive and bigger-brained competitors like the Cro-Magnon. It is why Mrs. Sabre-tooth and her progeny were unable to hunt us to extinction.

For evidence of a primal drive to connect with the rest of our kind, one need look no further than the unprecedented success of social networking.

We live in a harsh and unforgiving global business environment. It is tough to argue with the conviction that the organizations that will thrive – indeed, those that will survive will be those who liberate the natural curiosity that made us who we are.

The engagement paradox

Admittedly a dying species, there are still those who project an "I'm in charge, it's my way or or the highway" approach to leadership. When the job market favours the employer, when team members have little by way of portable skills, and when doing what we have always done is the name of the game, the notion that only one person should be "allowed to wind the clock" is a potential option – at least in the short term.

What those with autocratic tendencies tend to overlook is that the informal organization is far more influential than the dictates that come out of the corner office. What those wedded to a command-and-control approach fail to factor in is that fear doesn't build commitment, and a need to constantly ask permission isn't much of a blueprint for innovation. What they choose to ignore is those twins of business effectiveness – speed and simplicity (agility) – aren't formulaic; they are the outcome of giving people who do the work the opportunity to redesign how it gets done.

And here we bump into a twenty-first century paradox. A rejection by a new generation of the boomer's philosophy about work, that more and more employees now live in a different city (country) from the person to whom they report, a push for work–life balance, and a top-down recognition regarding the need to engage people have, indeed, over the past decade or so, changed the leadership conversation. The paradox: Overtures about the need to push decision making further into the organization haven't, as one might expect, necessarily resulted in a greater degree of discretion for one group of managers in particular.

Although many executives are genuinely wedded to the need for participation and involvement, they don't always help that cause. A combination of (1) the unprecedented loss of knowledge as the boomers

> *Although many executives are genuinely wedded to the need for participation and involvement, they don't always help that cause.*

retire,[73] (2) processes that are "engineered" to the point where judgment is taken out of the equation, and (3) the availability of ever-more sophisticated electronic tethers (e.g., BlackBerry, iPhone) means that middle managers, in particular, often have less freedom to make decisions than they did in the mid-nineties.[74]

The frustrating reality is that more and more executives are not only doing their own job but, through the magic of instant accessibility, they are making and/or backstopping many of the decisions that rightfully belong one or even two levels down. Intent and action are misaligned. A line from Michael Corleone in *The Godfather Part III* goes a long way to express the scenario being played out: "Just when I thought I was out, they pull me back in."

Fix the hole in the hull first

Perhaps the ultimate leadership challenge is to take a disparate group of individuals and turn them into a great team. Success can never be assured, but it's a challenge made easier if you know where to start.

Game playing is a common feature of underperforming teams.

Here pragmatism rules. If there is a hole in the boat, the team leader (or the leader one-level-up) **must** act quickly. You are up to your knees in water when, as the team leader, you are personally ill-equipped for the challenge, when one or more members on the team lack critical skills, when a key customer is disillusioned with someone who reports to you, when a member of the team is clearly a performance problem; or when it becomes apparent that a team member (often more than one) is "gaming the team."

Game playing is a common feature of underperforming teams. In some cases, the team itself becomes the game; where a malcontent member's covert disapproval[75] constantly derails the real work of the team. Gaming tends to follow one of the following themes:

> *"I know best."* A team member who appears to go along with what has been agreed upon, but then does their own thing anyway.

> *"We'll decide."* A small sub-group of the team decides ahead of time what they want to happen.

---

73 Research by Linda Duxbury at the University of Ottawa suggests that as two boomers retire they will have to be replaced by three non-boomers.

74 In the past two years, I have asked several hundred middle managers in different businesses if they had more freedom to act today than they had ten to fifteen years ago. Almost without exception, the answer was an emphatic "No!"

75 For "disapproval" read any combination of lack of self-confidence, anger, fear, anxiety, feelings of being unappreciated, or an inability to let go of past practice.

> *"No, you won't."* Conflict constantly bubbling away below the surface between two or more team members where deliberate barriers are thrown up or a lack of willingness to share knowledge inhibits the successful performance of the team overall.

> *"Yes, but ..."* When a team member regularly starts a sentence like this, the game is underway. What is about to unfold is non-supportive behaviour, where the real message is a variant of "I don't buy-in," "you're wasting my time," "it's not my job," "we've never done it that way," "I don't trust you," or "I'm way too busy." Little derails the team more successfully that a talented player who regularly "yes, buts" new ideas.

> *"We have the wrong leader."* A team member who goes out of their way to criticize the team leader outside of the team.

Game playing isn't limited to intact teams. Variations on these themes are not uncommon in team leader–subordinate relationships and in cross-functional teams. The dilemma: Failure to confront game playing communicates an assumed stamp of approval.

As for fixing the hole in the hull, I cannot ever recall a time when the leader, in looking back, said, "I moved too quickly."

The need to move beyond problem solving

Leaders at all levels have been trained and are, almost without exception, really good at one thing above all else: solving problems. Unfortunately, when it comes to teams, by doing what we have been trained to do, by relying on what we do best, by fixing what we perceive to be the problem, we can create (perpetuate) an even bigger problem.

Consider how leaders typically deal with a new team, a team that is struggling, or the need to move the team to the next level:

> **Step one** is for the team leader to move to the sidelines and "analyze" what isn't working. The focus: overt, easy-to-recognize behaviour that is clearly less than optimum. Typical concerns here are the need for greater collaboration, the need to improve the speed of action within and across the team, difficulty in letting go of past practices, members of the team who are either unwilling or don't know how to raise the performance bar, lack of focus in meetings, or buy-in during team meetings

but lack of follow-through. What gets overlooked is that symptom and cause are not necessarily the same thing. Working on the roof doesn't address a problem in the basement! What is ignored is that, faced with less-than-sterling team performance, the question any team leader should ask is, **"What do I need to do differently?"** If the team leader continues to do what he/she has always done, the team will likewise continue to act as they always have. Count on it!

> **Step two:** the seductive quick fix. What teambuilding session is out there that will help us address these issues? What one-day training event will make us whole? Where do I find the "expert" who can come in and sprinkle "pixie dust" on this dilemma?

> **Step three** is no less predictable. If, as is likely, the team leader discovers that there is no quick fix, the conversation inevitably moves from what's not working to who is to blame.

> **Step four:** constructive feedback to the "blocker(s)."

> **Step five:** separation of the problem children and, essentially, the creation of a new team.

A year later we are back on track. But not necessarily successfully back on track. Responding to observed behaviour is a seductive option but it doesn't always take account of the underlying factors that shaped **why** the team behaved the way it did; factors that may well, a year later, still influence how the "new" team deals with the world.

Assuming any holes in the hull have been plugged, there is an alternative place to begin, a way forward that recognizes that blowing up the team is a very expensive option.[76] What is being suggested is an approach to change that harbours the belief that the informal rules and approach to censure adopted by the team carry more weight than prescribed ways to behave that emanate from the formal hierarchy. Next steps build on the reality that motivation is always intrinsic (telling people they have to change doesn't work); that teams, when given the opportunity, are capable of finding their own way; and that, when inspired by a compelling purpose, even marginal employees can rise to become superstars. How many people does it take to change a light bulb? The number is irrelevant. The light bulb has to first want to be changed!

---

76 Here one needs to take account, not only of the cost of recruitment and the opportunity cost of recruitment lag, but also that the emerging market for talent means that finding top talent in the marketplace is going to become ever-more difficult.

For the team leader, it's all about mindset

The Greeks saw all nature as a living organism. They also viewed themselves not as dispassionate observers, but that nature was a reflection of themselves, and they were a reflection of nature. In other words, the observer and the observed were one and the same.

When viewed through the eyes of an observer, when seen as a series of standalone parts, the first question the leader asks when the team stumbles is inevitably, "What's broken?" When the team is viewed as a living system, smart leaders, as suggested earlier, focus initially on the one thing they can influence: **themselves.**

The conversation we have with ourselves defines who we are. We interpret the world by accessing the experiences encoded in our memory banks – by reassembling "what worked yesterday." A mechanistic mindset nurtures the belief that when someone new joins the team, like moving into a vacant parking spot, it is merely a matter of slotting that person into the "space" previously occupied. A holistic view reveals that every time a new team member is added – or taken away – we have, in essence, formed a new team[77] – a new team, moreover, that presents an opportunity to move beyond anything achieved in the past.

> *The conversation we have with ourselves defines who we are.*

When they look back, anyone who has had the privilege to be part of an exceptional team comes to realize that team success draws far more from the school of improvisation than it does from following a set script; that there are no stars, merely team members who have more lines than the others; and that, although each actor has a role to play, collaboration and the ability to self-organize are what really make the team special.

While on the topic, collaboration is how well-adjusted successful people with a common purpose and the freedom to make key decisions naturally work together. It is the default action. Where collaboration has to be forced, pushed, or mandated, something else is going on; something else is getting in the way.

We don't observe reality; we create our own reality. As a team leader, do you see the world through the eyes of a watchmaker, or is your way of acting echoed in the hum of the potter's wheel? Is the challenge perceived as replacing a broken part or taking the clay we have, adding or setting clay aside, but for the most part, shaping and drawing the

---

77 Merger and acquisition are legal terms. When two companies come together, a new organization always emerges.

potential out of that which is there? Is your approach to leadership defined by the problem in front of you, or is it, when everything else is stripped away, about the extent to which you inspire others to be the best they can be? Is it about attempting to push ever-harder, or about recognizing the need to work **SMART**er?

In a land where human clay is the most important resource you have, the potter reigns supreme! Five beliefs form the mind of the potter:

> **S**tart with the end in mind – you can't create what you can't imagine, and you can't deliver what you don't believe in.

> **M**astery is far more about how the artist approaches the work, than it is about the quality of the clay.

> **A** true artist works **with** the clay, not **on** the clay.

> **R**esonance, feel, and judgment are more important than imposed methodology.

> **T**rue excellence is an outcome of commercial insight, elegance of design, and fitness for purpose.[78]

You can't change the team by trying to change the team

Organizations on both sides of the Atlantic regularly engage in what is commonly referred to as "teambuilding." The unspoken truth behind these sessions is that, although they are often very engaging, more often than not, little changes.

Frustrated by the Molotov–Ribbentrop Pact in the prelude to World War II, Winston Churchill in an October 1939 broadcast described Russia as "a riddle wrapped in a mystery inside an enigma." Teams have many of those same exasperating qualities. The enigma that inhabits every team is that you can't change the team by trying to change the team.

We are driven to repeat "established patterns of play." When people attend a regular meeting, they want to sit in the same seat they previously occupied. Change is about breaking deep-rooted, defensive behaviour. It's about inspiring people. It's about striking the spark that makes people want to learn. The traditional business approach suggests everything will be okay if we take the time to provide feedback, teach new skills and, where deemed necessary, deliver formal "censure." Unfortunately, **telling** people that they must change leads to only

---

78 In January 2010, the Helsinki School of Economics, the University of Art and Design Helsinki, and the Helsinki University of Technology formed a new institution called Aalto University.

one likely outcome: an ongoing, emotional wrestling match that frustrates the heck out of everyone.[79]

What we learn from the neurosciences is that change is most effective when the intervention is at a higher level of abstraction than the behaviour we want to impact. Culture, mindset, ideas, values, beliefs, meaning, metaphor, and story – especially story! – thus become the prime movers of change.[80] New behaviour emerges, not when we focus on the behaviour, but when we build a new story, when we change the context, when the team leader acts differently, when we reframe the intrinsic motivation of those on the team. Teams are entirely capable of self-directed performance improvement. How they behave, however, is directly related to the environment the teams find themselves in. You can't change the team by trying to change the team, but you can change the conditions that lead them to act the way they do.

Work the context

Webster's dictionary defines context as "the set of circumstances or facts that surround a particular event or situation." Focusing on the immediate issue without considering the medium that surrounds that issue crops up all the time. A simple example is found in the way businesses, all too often, introduce coaching as a leadership practice. More than a few organizations quickly discover that it counts for naught to invest in excellent training if the organization's culture doesn't support a coaching mindset. The following examples speak to the power of context.

> *Teams are entirely capable of self-directed performance improvement.*

The first: a societal challenge that is part of all our lives – packaging and waste. Every two weeks, like many across North America, I leave my recycling at the curb for collection. Now, I will be the first to say that my local municipality has done an excellent job both with biological waste and everything recyclable. Indeed, their website indicates that truck journeys to the waste site are down several thousand a year. The downside is that a better system to identify, process, and recycle waste hasn't changed my basic buying habits. They have addressed the symptom but done little to influence the cause. If the truth be known, I probably buy more packaging than ever. Compare this to how Germany has

---

79 We need to be honest with people, but in the majority of cases, so-called constructive feedback, unless backed by life-changing consequences, rarely changes behaviour. Faced with either redefining who we are (our identity) or finding a reason why the feedback is unreasonable, we invariably opt for the latter.

80 Culture is story. Stories are how we make sense of the world. The stories we share shape how the team moves forward.

literally changed how people think about waste. The "tipping point" being that manufacturers and retailers in Germany carry the cost of much of the recycling; the more packaging there is, the higher the fees packaging and retail businesses are levied. Putting the burden on the manufacturers and sellers of packaging – changing the context – has led to less paper, thinner glass, and less metal being used. The outcome: a dramatic reduction in the amount of recyclable material consumers buy in the first place.

Then there is the remarkable success of Ocean Discovery Institute in San Diego. This non-profit institute uses scientific and environmental exploration to engage urban and diverse young people in three ways: education, scientific research, and environmental stewardship. Through their programs, youths drawn from low income areas, 38% of whom live below the poverty line, are challenged to transform their lives. They are not told to change, forced to change, and written off when they don't change. By reframing the context – by providing a new window on the world, by building on young people's instinctive attraction to the ocean, by focusing on possibility, by reframing how the students see themselves, they are inspired to learn. In discovering the world around them, these young people discover themselves. Moreover, by involving the students' own neighbourhoods in environmental projects, scientific literacy reaches a whole community. Nine out of ten of Ocean Discovery Institute's youth program graduates attend four-year universities, as compared to three out of ten of their peers. With a volunteer staff of over 300, during 2009, a total of 3,813 San Diego youth were provided with Ocean Discovery Institute programs on a tuition-free basis. The institute's target is to transform 20,000 young lives through science.

A third situation highlights what can happen when an attempt to enact change takes little heed of the wider context. Between 2002 and 2010, the US spent $6 billion dollars on developing the Afghan National Police (ANP) – a force that was desperately needed if the US and its allies were ever going to be able to exit Afghanistan. The money was spent on building police academies, arms, equipment, and training. The latter was provided by private security firms and delivered, for the most part, by ex-policemen. By all accounts, the $6 billion was totally wasted. This was not merely because many of the trainers were inadequately trained as trainers, but because 90% of the trainees were illiterate, 15% tested positive for drugs, and only a handful knew how to drive. Corruption, post-training attrition of 80%,[81] little or no trust from the local population, and lack of financial oversight merely added to

81   As of March 2010, out of 170,000 Afghans trained under the program, only 30,000 were still on the force.

the overall inefficiency.[82] In the rush to train an Afghan police force, someone forgot to ask the wider question, one rooted in the social and economic context: "Can the young men we are selecting actually be trained?" This is not an insignificant question; as reported in the Newsweek story,[83] between 2007 and early 2010, 1,000 Afghan Police officers "trained" under the program died as a result of firearm accidents and traffic collisions.

A final insight into the power of context comes from the best seller, *Freakonomics*.[84] The authors, Steven Levitt and Stephen J. Dubner, refer in some detail to the Early Childhood Longitudinal Study conducted by the US Department of Education in the late 1990s. Involving 20,000 children from all backgrounds, the research project looked at the relationship between academic performance and the home environment. Amongst the range of findings, one piece of data stands out. Test scores are influenced, not by whether the parents regularly read to their children, but whether "the child has many books in the home." The best way to get your children to read isn't to hire a tutor, it's to go out and buy some books.

The five things every team must know

For leaders seeking to take the team to the next level, working the context means, in the first instance, establishing the "trust triangle." (See Figure two.)

> *All relationships are about trust.*

All relationships are about trust. Trust is the glue that binds the disparate parts of the team into a cohesive whole. Trust is the "us" in business. Trust is the not-so-secret ingredient in innovation. That being said, trust is ultimately built (or lost) by delivering (or not delivering) on the promise. Teams that don't build trust represent an accident that hasn't been reported yet.

Trust is not just about relationships between members of the team. The genesis of team trust lies in how the rest of the organization views the team. Like fish swimming in water, the team is immersed in the wider organizational context. And like the fish, the team soon forgets that what surrounds them is literally the source of life. Pollute that life-giving force, introduce toxic elements, and sickness soon follows.

A healthy and supportive context (building organizational trust) is predicated on five things every team **MUST** know:

---

82   Mark Hosenball, Ron Moreau, and Mark Miller, "The Gang That Couldn't Shoot Straight," *Newsweek,* March 20, 2010.

83   *Newsweek,* March 20, 2010.

84   (Morrow, 2005), p. 167.

1. **The culture the wider organization is seeking to create.** Teams that fail to factor the emerging organizational culture into key decisions (e.g., hiring) are placing a blind bet on their own future. Teams that ignore tomorrow's culture are finessing themselves into a situation where the rest of the organization withdraws support.

   Although culture is far more than values, understanding the organization's values (guiding principles) is a team imperative. Values describe what has primacy. Values give people permission to act. Paradoxically, shared organizational values allow diversity to flourish. Assumptions that teamwork can move to higher ground without shared values is like expecting water to flow uphill. ***If you are the team leader:*** *Amplify the organization's values in all that you do.*

> *The most important person in any and every meeting – the customer – is absent. Great teams, as a result, are conscious of the need to make "the customer's voice" heard.*

   Any leader who, for a moment, thinks the organization's culture and values are not important should consider the accelerator pedal issues Toyota had to grapple with in 2010. Toyota's CEO, Akio Toyoda, in front of the US House Committee on Oversight and Government Reform, pointed out that Toyota's problems were a direct result of his organization moving away from its founding values (the Toyota Way).

2. **Why customers choose us and how that will change.** The most important person in any and every meeting – the customer – is absent. Great teams, as a result, are conscious of the need to make "the customer's voice" heard. But it has to be the real voice of the customer, not some stroked, groomed, and manicured consultant-driven synopsis. It has to reveal the underlying emotion behind why **your** customers choose you today and why **your** customers will want to work with you (or not) tomorrow.

   How the business makes money is ultimately about what the customer (1) wants to buy and (2) is willing to pay for it. Know also, for a fact, that both sides of that equation will change – in all likelihood, sooner than you have planned for. It matters not that the team is on the front-line or is a support group that has little opportunity to meet face-to-face with the customer; embedded in the DNA of every great team is a compelling need to understand the emerging need/price equation. ***If you are the team leader:*** *Learn everything you can about the customer's customer.*

The five things every team must know ...

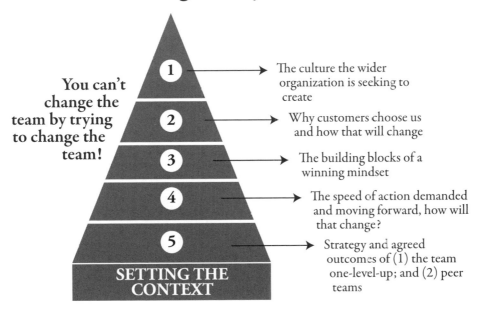

You can't change the team by trying to change the team!

1 → The culture the wider organization is seeking to create

2 → Why customers choose us and how that will change

3 → The building blocks of a winning mindset

4 → The speed of action demanded and moving forward, how will that change?

5 → Strategy and agreed outcomes of (1) the team one-level-up; and (2) peer teams

SETTING THE CONTEXT

Figure two   **The Trust Triangle**

3. **The building blocks of a winning mindset.** Great teams come to win. Winning is in their genes. It's simply how they are. That being said, a winning mindset isn't something that happens by accident. And although the team leader plays a key role, maintaining a will-to-win attitude is a state of mind everyone on the team must contribute to. This means:

› Recognizing that pride and a winning mindset are different sides of the same coin. A winning attitude isn't about merely beating the competition; for a great team, it's about burying the opposition. Few of us are inspired by the organization's attempts to move from #9 to #8 in their sector. It's not about size or past reputation – people simply want to be the best. If not in everything they do, at least in part of what they do.

› A degree of paranoia is both healthy and necessary. Fear reminds us that, somewhere in the business landscape, a competitor is figuring out how to do what we do faster and cheaper. Apprehension causes us to ask, "What's the worst thing the competition can do? Because we need to do it first." Anxiety indelibly etches into everyday conversation the certainty that constantly raising the bar is a fact of life. No less important, the right level of concern transforms desire into determination and insight into innovation. It shouldn't be assumed that fear and optimism are conflicting opposites. Winning lies in the tension drawn out of being, at the same time, both anxious and optimistic. In 1876 at the Battle of the Little Bighorn, US Colonel George Armstrong Custer threw away his own life and the lives of 268 of his men because he had way too much optimism and far too little anxiety.

> A talent acquisition process that always asks, "Will hiring this individual make us both a better team and a more successful organization?"

> Champions, when the need arises, change the game. Any team member wedded to doing things the way they have always been done belongs on a different team.

> "Winning without integrity isn't winning." At the end of the 1941 US baseball season, Ted Williams, the Boston Red Sox hall-of-famer was hitting .3995 batting average. If he had sat out the last game, as his manager suggested, that would have been rounded up to .400. His view of winning, however, didn't include coasting to the batting title. So instead of sitting out the game, he played in a double-header against the Oakland A's, went six-for-eight, and actually finished the season with an even better average of .406. Now that's winning **with** integrity! No player has hit .400 since.

No matter how elegant the processes, no matter how much effort and energy goes into building collaborative relationships – if the team lacks the passion to win, runner-up is the best that can be hoped for. *If you are the team leader:* *Be optimistic.*

4. **The speed of action demanded to succeed and, moving forward, how that will change.** It took 70 years for electricity to become ubiquitous; 50 years for the telephone; 30 years for television; 10 years for the Internet; and only three years for Facebook to go from start-up to 350 million users.[85] No matter how one thinks about the future, one fact is non-negotiable: The speed at which change is being enacted (velocity) is increasing at a rate hitherto unknown.[86] Assuming that the clock speed of the organization is tied to past practice is the management

---

85   Facebook added 250 million users between August 2008 and December 2009. By June 2010, the number of users reached 500 million.

86   The one exception is the rate at which printing spread across Europe. Between 1452, when Gutenberg printed his first bible, and 1500, some 2,500 European cities introduced their own printing presses. Twenty million books were printed during that time – 77% of them in Latin.

equivalent of taking a knife to a gunfight. Setting the scene for extraordinary team performance must take account of, and proactively set in motion, the behaviour, processes, and technology needed to live in a world addicted to moving ever-faster. *If you are the team leader: Model, in everything you do, the speed of action you need the team to adopt.*

5. **The strategy and agreed-upon outcomes of (a) the team one-level-up and (b) peer teams.** One of the measures of excellence in sports is that a great player makes those around him/her "up their game." Great teams come to win. They are also conscious of the fact that winning the game but losing the championship is a hollow victory.

    If you are the team leader: Know that no team can thrive in a vacuum and that a mutualistic, symbiotic relationship with other key teams is the only game in town. Keep all your colleagues in the loop.

Without working the Trust Triangle, without institutional trust, without a sense of being connected to the larger whole, without considering the context, what must inevitably emerge is the team version of "good news, bad news." The good news: We are making great time. The bad: We are lost!

The easy option isn't always the best option. If your son can't read, buying him a new book doesn't help much. Changing the players will result in a new squad, but it doesn't necessarily change the game.

Change needs a spark. It needs a catalyst. Indeed, before much of anything is possible, the seeds of possibility have to be sown. And here, gardeners know what business leaders often overlook. You can't just throw the seeds on the ground and expect growth. You have to prepare the ground, till the soil, provide nutrients, and water as needed.

You can't change the team by trying to change the team. You have to work the context. You have to bring the right nutrient to the team and yes, metaphorically, water as needed. To prepare the ground, you must act on the five things every team most know. As for adding the life-sustaining water, to lead is to care. *If you are the team leader: People on the team need to know that you care.*

YOU CAN'T CHANGE THE TEAM BY TRYING TO CHANGE THE TEAM

If the leaders across my organization really knew how to get the best out of the teams they manage, we would:

_____

_____

_____

_____

_____

As an organization, to move from the mind of the watchmaker to the mind of the potter, we have to:

_____

_____

_____

_____

_____

Starting now, to get the best out of my team, I will:

_____

_____

_____

_____

_____

_____

Chapter five:
TAKING THE TEAM TO THE NEXT LEVEL

In an upside-down world

In the recent past, when the team appeared to be stuck, the ubiquitous retreat, the so-called teambuilding workshops, and any number of consultant-driven interventions were often deemed to be the best way forward. Teams grow, not because they pursue the elixir of a quick fix, but because the team leader orchestrates a systematic way to move the team through the different stages of team development. In other words, taking the team to the next level isn't an intervention, it's not a project, and it's not something that can be delegated to a consultant. Successful leaders work to draw the best out of those around the table every single day.

The narrative of the trapped mind

"Let's bring someone in to run a teambuilding session."

"What we really need to develop is a 'results-driven culture.'" (Because the focus is on results, what tends to be enacted is a beefed-up approach to the performance management process with scant regard to the "culture" needed to drive results, e.g., candour.)

"I don't believe I personally need to do anything differently. I hired these people. I am the team leader. My role is to fix this thing."

"If there are team roles missing, I can bridge any shortfall."

"Perhaps I do need to become an inspirational presence. It would help if my own boss inspired me."

The rest of the story …

The DNA of the team is a double helix: two tightly entwined strands containing the information needed to excel.

Taking the team to the next level

"To build the muscle needed to break through the barriers erected from past practice, the medium that surrounds the team has to support and nurture a new way to be."

The team is a complex bundle of energy, ideas, personalities, dreams, assumptions, and self-imposed norms. It is a living system. And as with any system, change any single element and you change the whole. The dilemma: First-order change – working on parts of the system, a "let's fix what (or who) is broken" mentality – is not only ineffective but, in many cases, carries the added burden of building silent and often lasting resentment. Simply put: You can't change the team by trying to change the team! (See Chapter four.)

To build the muscle needed to break through the barriers erected from past practice, the medium[87] that surrounds the team has to support and nurture a new way to be. Second-order change – working on the whole system, shaping the context, bridging the aspirations of the team with the culture of the wider organization, reframing mindsets, redefining the team's story, and bringing the organization's values to life – offers an integrity-laden approach that builds lasting change.

> *Working with the team as a whole system demands a holistic mindset.*

Not much of anything happens, of course, without leadership. How the leader turns up profoundly influences how things unfold. To lead is to believe. To lead is to plug into the energy that thrives in the white space between the boxes on the organization chart. To lead is to have the courage to let go of a mechanistic mindset.

Working with the team as a whole system demands a holistic mindset. It is predicated on a recognition that the DNA of the team is a double helix: two tightly entwined strands containing the information needed to excel. One strand contains the blueprint describing strategy, results, and priorities. The other, the relationships demanded if team members are to draw the best out of each other – if trust is to flourish. Teams that consistently deliver what others say cannot be done give equal weight to both outcomes and relationships. Brought to life by an inspirational leader,[88] the "performance double helix" represents the heartbeat of a truly great team. (See Figure three.)

---

87 The "medium" is a liquid or gel designed to support the growth of cells.

88 See page 43.

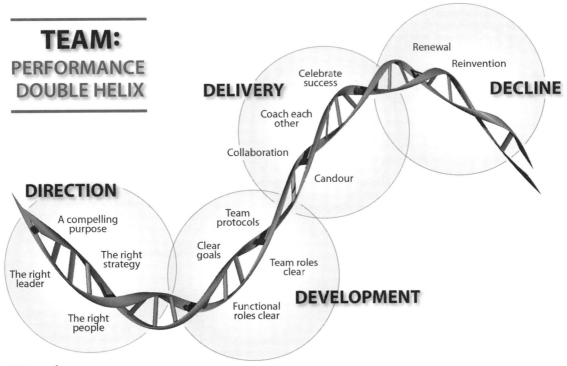

TEAM:
PERFORMANCE
DOUBLE HELIX

DIRECTION

DELIVERY

DECLINE

DEVELOPMENT

Renewal

Reinvention

Celebrate
success

Coach each
other

Collaboration

Candour

A compelling
purpose

The right
strategy

Clear
goals

Team
protocols

Team roles
clear

The right
leader

The right
people

Functional
roles clear

Figure three

Although every team is unique, experience suggests that the growth of the team follows a sigmoidal curve. [89] As the team seeks **direction,** as those who influence the team strive to bring the right people to the challenge, performance is less than optimum. Next is a **development** stage: a series of steps that defines roles and responsibility, the results demanded, and how the team is going to work together as a team. **Delivery** follows, but only if characteristics such as candour, collaboration, and celebrating success start to emerge.[90] **Decline**[91] and the need for renewal and, in some instances, reinvention complete the sigmoid.

The following questions track the performance double helix. The questions should not be perceived as standalone issues – as disconnected strings to be pulled. They are presented as initial steps on the passage to excellence and, as the journey unfolds, as a pallet of ideas to be blended and remixed as need suggests.

---

89 Shaped like the letter S.

90 A level of capability often described as "a high-performance team."

91 In an ideal world, the time to reinvent the team is before decline sets in.

Is there a compelling purpose?

It starts with the purpose – Why are we here? The purpose is what makes people get up in the morning with a spring in their step. It's why people who could earn more money elsewhere, stay. It's what gives the work meaning. If those on the team aren't connected to the team's purpose, self-interest becomes the only game in town.

Danny Blanchflower, the articulate Irish soccer legend, in response to a question about "desire" answered, "Winning isn't everything, but wanting to is!"[92] Without a compelling purpose, it's all but impossible to build a winning mindset.

The purpose is to the team what the North Star is to navigation: It illuminates. It is the compass bearing to steer by. It is a touchstone the team can return to when doubt enters the conversation. A team without a compelling purpose is becalmed, a sailing ship trying endlessly to catch the wind.

Unfortunately, in most teams, the purpose comes across as bland and lifeless. By comparison, in a high-energy, responsive, customer-facing team the purpose is a source of inspiration. To that end, it's not enough to merely state the purpose.

A successful leader takes people on a journey; through rich and imagery-filled language, a leader makes the desired destination live in people's hearts. The capacity to do this describes an ability to paint a word picture of the future with such clarity and detail that tomorrow's success becomes part of how everyone on the team and everyone associated with it views tomorrow's reality. Members of the team have to own the purpose; they have to be able to see and touch what it looks and feels like when it's enacted (future state). Walt Disney said it best: "If you can dream it, you can do it. Always remember that this whole thing was started with a dream and a mouse."

The best leaders keep it simple. The "compelling purpose," as presented here, folds mission, vision, and purpose into one single, vibrant, emotionally-laden, mental picture of tomorrow's success. Although useful when considering the organization overall, at the level of the team the distinction between mission, vision, and purpose has the potential to unnecessarily confuse people.

If you are the team leader: Reject a statement of purpose (written or otherwise) that doesn't inspire you personally. Harness the imagination of the team. People are committed

---

92   Also attributed to Vince Lombardi, the legendary American football coach.

to what they create. They fight for what lives in their hearts. Have the team write a letter to itself dated a year from now. The letter should highlight all the things that have been achieved looking back over the "past" year in pursuit of the team's purpose. In that we cannot distinguish between mental rehearsal and the real thing, watching success unfold in the mind makes it far more likely it will happen in real life. Write a new letter a year from now.

If you are the team leader: *Fold the team's purpose into a compelling story. The building blocks of a great organization story were described in Chapter three. They are worth revisiting from a team perspective:*

1. Where is the team heading?

2. What do we believe in?

3. What makes the team special?

4. How does what we do within the team make a difference in people's lives?

Know that a compelling purpose (a great story) is the genesis of trust.

Does the team have the right leader?

Team members **need** (not want) four things from a leader:[93]

1. A clear sense of where the team is heading (**the head**).

2. The discipline of delivery (**the hand**).

3. To draw out the best from everyone on the team (**the heart**).

4. That the leader be a positive and caring role model (**the spirit**).

To come up short in any one of these is, in a real sense, to fail them all.

The question I am often asked is, "Where does intelligence play a role in leadership success?" The head, hand, heart, spirit leadership model describes four different forms of intelligence. **The head** is clearly about cognitive intelligence and the capacity to deal with complexity. **The hand** is all about delivery and the organizational savvy needed to get things done – what is often referred to as "street smarts." **The heart** is about inter-personal intelligence (working with others). **The spirit**, meanwhile, is about intra-personal intelligence (knowing ourselves). (See Figure four.)[94]

---

93 "The head, the hand, the heart, and the spirit" template is based on facilitated sessions in over 25 countries and with over 10,000 leaders. See also my book *New Role, New Reality* (Executive Forum, 2000).

94 Based on discussions with over 10,000 leaders in 25 countries.

WHAT PEOPLE NEED FROM A LEADER

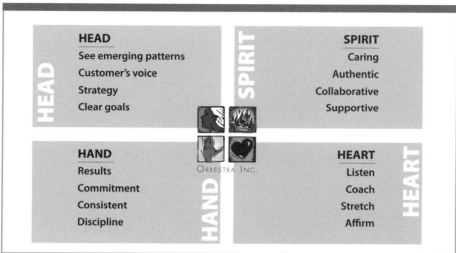

Figure four

A fifth intelligence is growing in importance and needs to also be factored in: "societal intelligence" (our footprint on the wider society, e.g., the environment). Daniel Goleman, who introduced us all to the term "emotional intelligence," calls this "ecological intelligence." Much like those cardboard containers in a Chinese restaurant take-out, societal intelligence folds itself around the other four intelligences identified. We have lost touch with what our aboriginal cousins still make the centre of their very existence. Indeed, societal intelligence may well prove to be the most important of the five dimensions of intelligence – if we are to survive the next 200 years as a species, that is.

> *Leaders who inspire employ the head, empower the hand, engage the heart, and enrich the spirit.*

Leaders who inspire employ the head, empower the hand, engage the heart, and enrich the spirit. What makes them special, however, is that they don't stop there – they go deeper. (See Figure five.)

1. They **communicate** with a richness of language such that emerging patterns in the marketplace are translated into tangible opportunities; the customer is an ever-present "member" of the team; the strategy becomes a persuasive call to action; and the key goals are crystal clear. *To inspire is to bring the dream to life.*

TO INSPIRE:

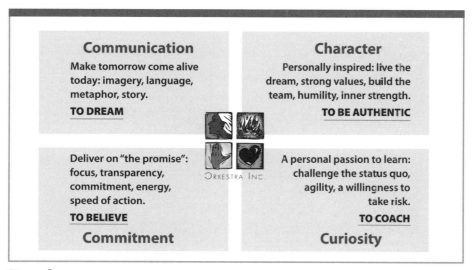

Figure five

2. They display an unwavering **commitment** to the outcomes demanded such that no one is in any doubt that it **will** – not could, might, or should – happen. *To inspire is to believe!*

3. An extension of an innate and seemingly insatiable **curiosity** about the world around them, they have a passion to learn and share that learning with others. Challenging the way things are is thus simply a way to be. *To inspire is to be a great coach/mentor.*

4. At the very core of who they are, ingrained in every fibre of their **character**, is that they are personally inspired by the challenge ahead. *To inspire is to be authentic!*

It's interesting to add that inspirational leaders, especially those on the national stage, often use symbolism and theatrical gestures to make their message more appealing. One immediately thinks of Hitler and his ability (at least, before his invasion of Russia, after which he went into isolation) to come across as one of the people – by dressing down. This only worked, of course, because his entourage were encouraged to dress in magnificent uniforms dripping with medals. Mussolini kept crowds waiting for hours in the heat of the day before making a speech. With the setting sun in the background, his sudden, and by now much anticipated appearance apparently transformed the delirious and weary mob into an adoring crowd. No doubt, you had to be there! In the meantime, Churchill had his cigar and victory sign and Roosevelt his elaborate cigarette holder. The modern-day use of theatrics can be seen in Richard Branson's stunts, Steve Job's black turtleneck sweater, and Sergio Marchionne's ever-present, dark-coloured Italian sweater[95] with its obligatory small Italian flag on one sleeve.

In an ideal world, the team leader will be the inspirational presence the team needs. Sadly, the ability to inspire is a leadership capability that few organizations have in abundance. Where the team leader is inexperienced, chosen largely because of technical expertise, or a poor communicator, inspiration (at least initially) has to come from the leader one-level-up.

Important as inspiration is, the leader's perceived capability is no less impactful on the team. Know that the only thing that melts faster than a snowball on a summer's day is the team's commitment when presented with a leader who, they perceive, lacks the qualities needed to get the job done. That frustration is compounded when the leader's behaviour suggests any indication of arrogance.

The team leader must inspire the team. The leader must also be a fit with the work to be done. This is ultimately a matter of being "the right horse for the course." There are five "courses" to take into account:

1. Start-up.

2. Growing a business beyond the start-up phase.

3. Taking a mature business to the next level.

4. Delivering on a business turnaround.

5. Transforming the culture.

Fuelled by imagination and entrepreneurial drive, leaders who regularly succeed in a business start-up are a rare breed.

Meanwhile, leaders who take a start-up business to the next stage understand that success is predicated on growing the people. Who to hire and how to coach is what ultimately differentiates the winners from those who merely make a good showing.

Taking a mature business to the next level involves that rare combination of cost containment **and** growth; consolidation **and** innovation; honouring the past **and** creating a new tomorrow; delighting established customers **and** entering new markets; managing the culture **and**, at the same time, evolving the culture.

---

95   Much to the chagrin of the Italian fashion industry, Marchionne wears his sweaters over a shirt and no tie.

Scarce are those executives who can deliver business turnaround. Assuming business turnaround is demanded, faced with a choice between a leader with little or no track record of successful turnarounds and selling the business, the latter is by far the best choice. One is money in the hand, the other is a prohibitively expensive, on-the-job training program.

As for transforming the culture, only a superbly trained and highly experienced thoroughbred has any chance whatsoever of finishing the race. Few leaders who wax lyrical about the need to "change the culture" understand what's really involved (have done it before), have the capacity to inspire those in the middle of the organization, or possess the stamina needed to stay the course.

The leader sets the tone, builds a sense of urgency, energizes the team when enthusiasm flags, and establishes performance standards by personally setting the bar extraordinarily high. An outstanding leader is the arbiter of fairness, the guardian of consistency and, in an echo of the US Marine Corps, the first one to step foot on the battlefield and the last one to leave. And yes, outstanding leaders go out of their way to make sure no one is left behind.

I really can't move on without reference to those extraordinary leaders who not only inspire, who not only transform but who, in doing so, leave a lasting legacy. What is it that makes them different? Do they work through the head, hand, heart, and spirit? Absolutely. A high level of cognitive intelligence? Certainly. That they are smart enough to know how to get things done – it can be taken for granted. That they possess, both inter- and intra-personal intelligence – unquestionably. There is something else, however. Beyond the qualities mentioned there is a difficult-to-define "X" factor. Like an oyster where the grain of sand is the catalyst, my own experience is that those rare leaders who truly change the world around them are driven by an inner yearning, a fire that cannot be extinguished, a voice that cannot be silenced. This life-force is more than motivation, more than the drive to win – it's what amounts to a compulsion. For some it's about filling an emotional void. With others it's an unanswered question that fills their every waking hour. A third group push everything else aside in a passion-filled quest to find their Holy Grail – that Joseph Campbell described as "following your bliss."[96] Do they have flaws? Beauty isn't to be without a blemish. It's about perfection complemented by a flaw. To paraphrase Friedrich Nietzsche, *I tell you: One must have chaos within oneself, to give birth to a dancing star.*

---

96   Joseph J. Campbell (1904–1987), American writer and lecturer, best known for his enduring work in mythology.

How much does it cost to have the wrong leader in place? Bradford D. Smart in his book, *Topgrading*, suggests the real cost of an executive mis-hire to be 28 X the base salary.[97] In his exacting study of mis-hires, where the average base compensation for executives earning between $100,000 and $250,000, was $168,000, the negative cost to the organization for each hiring mistake was, on average, $4,707,000, for a minus 500% ROI.

If you are the team leader: Be honest with yourself about what you are, and are not, equipped to do. Reach out for support where it is needed. Work from the presumption that involving people in the decision is the best way to gain buy-in. Be humble. Ask for feedback early and often. Recognize that nothing you do is as important as the simple act of listening. And know that if you don't extend trust, you can't build trust.

Does the team have the right strategy?

There is a big difference between strategic thinking and strategic planning. Today's organizations tend to be blessed with a surfeit of the latter while being somewhat impoverished in the former. To be a successful team leader is to be accomplished in both.

Uncertain times means that strategic leadership is less about analysis than it is about interpreting the emerging patterns – before your toughest competitor can figure it out. It means, by implication, that the direction agreed on isn't set in stone and that "the strategy" is always being fine-tuned, modified, and, where necessary, recast to reflect the emerging business realities.

> *Successful leaders recognize the symbiotic relationship between, and invest equally in, both strategy and culture.*

An unpredictable world also throws greater weight than ever on the relationship between strategy and culture. Successful organizations strive to create both a strong and an agile culture (StrAgility).[98] Strength speaks to focus. Agility is all about building the capacity for different strategic scenarios to unfold. If you commanded forces opposing a Roman Legion, you were first confronted with the strength of their "shield wall." Shortly thereafter you became painfully aware of how agile the razor sharp, 26-inch gladius (65 cm. short sword) enabled their first line to be. Great organizations, like great teams, embrace StrAgility.

Leaders who work from the assumption that strategy drives culture (agree on the strategy and then build the culture to support that strategy) are destined to struggle. Culture isn't

---

97 *Topgrading* (Penguin, 2005), p. 50.

98 See *Myth, Magic, Mindset* (2008). The conclusion to the book is my "StrAgility" questionnaire: To what extent is your organization's culture both (1) strong and (2) agile?

something you work on after defining the strategy. Successful leaders recognize the symbiotic relationship between, and invest equally in, both strategy and culture. A bicycle with one wheel is not only difficult to ride; it's of little or no use when you get to the first steep hill.

Strategic thinking and strategic planning represent the first two vectors of the strategic triangle. The third is strategic implementation: an action orientation that speaks not just to having a great plan, but consistently delivering on that plan.

If you are the team leader: Four imperatives frame strategic implementation:

Set targets that build on people's strengths.

Hold people accountable – and always follow through.[99]

Instill a sense of urgency.

Provide support if unforeseen problems arise.

In recent decades, both popular management writers and leading academics have emphasized the importance of having the right strategy. Unfortunately, in doing so they have discounted the importance of strategic implementation. Evidence suggests that an outstanding leader with no plan or even the wrong plan is still likely to find a way to deliver value. Meanwhile, an elegant plan that isn't implemented clearly isn't worth the paper it's printed on.

President Truman, when asked about General Grant's success in the Civil War, said, "Grant had a very ... simple idea about winning the war. He wasn't much ... he didn't know much about strategy. A lot of the other generals on both sides, they had all studied the same books at West Point and ... Grant, he wasn't much of a scholar or writer. Grant said, 'What you have to do to fight a war, you have to find the enemy, and you have to hit him with everything you've got. And then you have to keep right on going.'"[100]

If you are the team leader: *Be passionate about execution. There is a reason it's called leader-S-H-I-P. Know that not to deliver is not to be trusted.*

Does the team have the right people?

When we bring someone new onto the team, there is an opportunity to enhance team performance and build bench strength. To that end, hiring is a make-or-break process. It is surprising, therefore, how few leaders truly know how to successfully evaluate potential "fit."

---

99   In *Execution: The Discipline of Getting Things Done* (Crown, 2002), Larry Bossidy and Ram Charan write that "follow-through" is the cornerstone of execution (p.127).

100 Merle Miller, *Plain Speaking: An Oral Biography of Harry S. Truman* (Berkley, 1974), p. 312.

It's not that those same individuals don't recognize the importance of hiring the right person. Intent, yes. Successful execution, not always![101] The concern: "Practice" doesn't necessarily equate to know-how. And anything less than genuine expertise, when it comes to hiring and retaining talent, is to short-change the team and everyone involved.

The ten questions that follow cut to the very essence of successful talent acquisition. A response of "somewhat" or "some of the time" to any single question suggests that there is work to be done:

1. Is it clear **why talented people stay** with the organization or team? Retention has to be at the very core of any and all hiring and promotion decisions.

2. Does the organization or team have **a compelling story** that engages people emotionally? You can't hire the best unless you attract the best!

3. Is **talent scouting** part of how the business does business? Talent scouting, in turn, describes the ability to monitor the marketplace generally; the means to identify potential successors for key roles amongst leaders who do not currently work within the business; and the capability to bring high-potential talent into the organization although there may not be a specific role available at the time.

4. Is **performance fit** measured against a well-thought-through scorecard for the role in question?

5. Is **cultural fit** central to the hire decision? This implies the means to measure both the current culture and the culture the organization is seeking to create.

6. Is **leadership fit** measured against role-specific competencies? The key term is "role-specific." Generic competencies are needed to evaluate fit with the organization overall, but the assumption that, for example, a key sales role in an established business shares the same leadership competencies as an R&D position in a business start-up is less than helpful.

7. Is **team fit** front and centre in the hiring decision? This implies a means to assess both the stage of development of the team and the contribution (in addition to functional performance) of each member to the team.

8. Is it understood that generally, but especially insofar as performance fit is concerned, traditional behavioural interviewing is an inappropriate tool for

---

101 John E. Hunter of Michigan State University suggested that the typical interview has only a 57% chance of predicting employment success in the long term.

assessing Gen X, Gen Y, and those now entering the job market for the first time?[102] The way forward: an **evidence-based approach** where experience is matched against the specific demands and outcomes of the role (e.g., scorecard).

9. Is there a highly-lauded, **comprehensive, self-managed process** that enables those moving onto the team to land without breaking stride? Know, if they don't land they won't stay!

10. Has the organization **partnered with external groups** (e.g., executive search organizations) who can bridge any shortfalls that are evident in any of these criteria?

Clearly, it's essential that anyone brought onto the team is carefully assessed with regards to performance, culture, leadership, and team fit. Given that the business environment changes, it is no less important that established team members are periodically assessed against standards that are no less exacting. Not to do so is to invite "Mr. Complacency" and his best buddy "Ms. Status Quo" onto the team.

If you are the team leader: Regularly assess your overall capability against the key dimensions of fit described. Engage a third party to regularly audit the effectiveness of the hiring process. With the same goal in mind, solicit the opinion of, and listen to, those who have recently joined the team. Know that if capability (fit) is found wanting, trust takes a vacation.

Are the functional roles clear?

The late Sir Thomas Beecham, the English conductor, was leading his orchestra through a complex piece that, at a critical point, called for an off-stage trumpet call. Except, when the moment arrived ... there was no trumpet. His first response: simply repeat the passage. Except ... there was still no trumpet. The great man threw down his baton and strode purposefully to the side of the stage to find out what the culprit was up to. What he discovered was his aforementioned trumpet player in the embrace of a very burly security guard who was insisting with some force, "You can't play that damn trumpet here, there's a concert going on."[103]

It's not enough that each member of the team understand their own role. The rest of the people on the team and, indeed, the wider team, have to understand what that role is.

---

102 The market savvy of these cohorts means that they will anticipate, and in most instances have already rehearsed, the response the interviewer is looking for.

103 I first came across a version of this story in a book entitled *Team Power* by Thomas A. Kayser. p. 57.

"The job" describes tasks and outcomes measured against predetermined standards. To that end, "the job" drives the individual and, regardless of the incumbent, the measure of success remains the same.

"A role," on the other hand, describes core areas of responsibility and authority that capture the requisite[104] demands of the position. Outside of that requisite core lies an area of influence shaped by the capability of the individual in the role. In a role, each individual moulds the nature of their overall contribution.

It quickly becomes apparent that, as an individual expands their contribution outside of the core, we move into a world where areas of influence overlap – and not just between members of the same team. The capability that team members bring to managing these zones of overlapping influence defines the very essence of what makes a successful team. A team member with limited competency in building a constituency, who lacks interpersonal skill in managing internal networks, or who has a built-in propensity to build walls rather than relationships, is unable to fully contribute to the growth of the team.

> *Everyone on the team has two roles: functional and team.*

Defining the requisite scope of the role gives permission to act. It is no less important that every team member work from the mindset that requisite authority and responsibility merely describe where the role begins. Without an ability to develop and draw value out of the informal arenas of overlapping influence, today's team member is destroying tomorrow's possibility.

If you are the team leader: Challenge assumptions that even hint at "turf" or "it's not my job." Both model and emphasize the value of collaboration. Highlight success drawn out of innovation and unbundle how that success was enacted. Engage the team in a conversation about what you personally can do to get out of the way. Regularly revisit what you need to let go of. Know that when the capacity for growth is lost, lack of trust is the cost.

Are the "team roles" clear?

Everyone on the team has two roles: functional and team. The setting for the functional role has already been discussed. The contribution each person makes to team success is no less important. Here, my own work with top teams has convinced me that there are six distinct

---

104 That which, regardless of circumstances or opportunity, must be accomplished.

team roles – behaviour that, if not part of how the team thinks and acts, handicaps team performance:[105]

1. **Visionary:** an individual who can see over the horizon but, while doing so, through vibrant and emotion-laden language, brings future possibility to life. Without a visionary the team is lost.

2. **Explorer:** a team member who makes and, where necessary, pushes for the business case; easily identified by depth of market experience and commercial savvy. A team without an explorer is likely to end up with a great product that no one knows about or a service that goes to market at the wrong price.

3. **Pioneer:** what the visionary can see and the explorer knows how to fund, this individual creates through innovation and breakthrough thinking. Without a pioneer, you are destined to be a follower. Without a pioneer, you're selling a commodity.

4. **Warrior:** no matter the product or service, someone has to sell, deliver, and service it. Without a warrior(s), the team is likely to remain a collection of individuals with a great idea.

5. **Maverick:** without challenge, without tough questions, without someone to ask, "Is there a better way?" even outstanding teams get trapped by yesterday's success. Without a maverick, sacred cows graze with impunity.

6. **Navigator:** the team member who provides the map enabling the team to move into new territory; who challenges the language and metaphors used; who holds up a mirror and helps the team better understand how they operate. Without a navigator, team learning is held back, unhelpful language seeps into the conversation, and the stories the team should be sharing remain untold.

Although teams in the middle of the organization may have members who can fulfill different team roles, the closer one comes to the apex of the organizational pyramid, the less likely it is that any individual will display true mastery in more than one role. When you look across the team, are all the roles outlined present? If not, how can you address that shortfall?

If you are the team leader: Understand the role on the team at which you excel. Don't strive to become something you are not. Address role shortfalls by inviting talented individuals to join

---

105 Taken from my book *Leaders Must Lead!* (2003).

the team as the situation demands. Don't expect 100% involvement from every team member all the time. Extroverts are energized through interaction. Introverts need time and space to process what has been said. Know that when a key role isn't represented, the chemistry needed for trust to become truly part of the ethos of the team is missing a critical element.

Are the performance goals clear?

Does everyone on the team have stretch objectives for their roles? Are those agreed-upon outcomes unambiguous? Are they attainable, few in number, and aligned with the individual's strengths? Does every team member have one goal that stretches beyond this fiscal year?

Are team members full partners in creating those goals? As part of the goal setting is it clearly understood how the customer (end-user) will benefit? Is it understood that goals, once agreed upon, are a personal commitment and that failure to deliver carries consequences?

Self-management is enabled when the team leader builds a scorecard with each member of the team. A meaningful scorecard sets out (1) the financial goals and (2) the areas of value creation that roll up to deliver the agreed-upon financial outcomes. There are four areas of value creation: (a) operational value (e.g., driving down operating costs); (b) market-facing value (e.g., growing the customer base); (c) people value (e.g., succession planning); and (d) social value (e.g., sustainability). Integrated into a business intelligence system, a scorecard approach is an excellent method of monitoring overall business performance.

There's an old adage: "What you measure is what you get." By rewarding that which is measured, leaders strip uncertainty out of the performance equation. Pushing for collaboration and then rewarding individual effort is but one example of the compensation system working against desired outcomes. Something similar occurs when it comes to the organization's values. It is meaningless to emphasize the need for every leader to be committed to the "organization's values" and then skew the performance management system such that the only thing that really matters is the result achieved.

If you are the team leader: *Balance the long- and the short-term. Learn to love (simple) scorecards. Establish agreed milestones for both individual and team goals. Review both as a team. Follow up. Benchmark against the best. Know that when team members don't know what's expected of them, trust is an early victim.*

Have team protocols been agreed on?

It is not enough for the team to meet the goals outlined. To be successful, the team must capture what was learned from the experience. Learning also points towards the team having clearly defined and agreed upon measures of team success.

Teams are successful when (1) they deliver results and (2) when they continue to grow as a team (team process).[106] A focus on one to the exclusion of the other is to ultimately limit the effectiveness of both. Setting goals that focus on business outcomes is a given. This is not so for agreed-upon criteria that establish when the team – as a team – is successful. Surprisingly few teams agree on the protocols (a set of simple rules) that describe how the team and, by implication everyone on the team, agrees to behave. And yet, if success "of the team" is allowed to remain a hit-or-miss affair, candour, feedback, and growth become all but impossible to orchestrate.

Criteria for team success typically embrace five to eight simple statements of intent, statements that tend to focus on issues such as these:

> "Every member of the team is heard."
>
> "We challenge what is said, but we don't criticize the speaker."
>
> "We have simple guidelines for decision making."
>
> "We honour the confidentiality of team meetings."
>
> "We follow an agreed-upon process for generating new ideas."

Teams that know-together, grow-together. Without ongoing learning, risk becomes an act of last resort and not, as it should be, a judgment call that draws on wisdom grounded in past experience.

Learning is benchmarking against the best. It is a willingness to be at the edge. It means taking time out for reflection. It demands openness. It implies knowing specifically how to support someone new to the team. It involves rallying round when a colleague faces a difficult challenge. It is all about building on the team's strengths – not constantly worrying about the small things that don't always go right.

> *A team without candour is a team without can-do.*

---

106 The double helix.

If you are the team leader: Have the team review behaviour against the agreed-upon protocols regularly.[107] Insist that team members act on the insights that come out of those conversations. Understand that how people on the team work together has a profound impact on results. Know that change and learning are but different ways to say the same thing. Know that when the protocols are left unspoken, the potential to build trust remains unfulfilled.

Is candour part of the mix?

A team without candour is a team without can-do. Being part of a great team isn't necessarily a comfortable experience. To be a leader is to love diversity and embrace ambiguity. It is to nurture the maverick on the team. It is to speak up even when others suggest that the expedient thing would be to remain silent. It is to eschew game playing and recognize that the "dead moose" lying in the middle of the table won't go away no matter how much one tries to ignore it. It is to be sensitive to the needs of others but to challenge their way to see the world even if it makes them uncomfortable.

When the "undiscussable" lies hidden, when what isn't said becomes the focus of the team's collective mind, ideas and possibilities get trapped behind an impenetrable wall of self-imposed silence.

If you are the team leader: Be the first to ask the tough question. Build emotional energy for the difficult conversation by supporting those who speak out. Make candour a way of life. Know that without candour, trust becomes little more than a fleeting image of what is possible.

Is collaboration alive and well?

Although much of the literature would have us believe otherwise, collaboration is far more a state of mind than it is a set of techniques dependent upon emerging technology. It is simply the natural way that *Homo sapiens* think and act – an outcome of who we are as a species that, in an organizational setting, is enabled by the following:

"**C**an-do" defines the dominant mindset. The enemy of collaboration is any conversation that involves language along the lines of "It's not our job," "We've never done it that way," "If only we had ... ," or "We don't have the time."

Organization support is ever-present. By "support" is implied a flat structure, a drive

---

107 Some teams are committed to spending a short time at the end of every meeting to discuss how they behaved as a team.

to simplify key processes, that employees know what is going on, and that time and space is set aside for employees at all levels to reinvent possibility without imposed boundaries getting in the way.[108]

Learning is a way of life. Learning in the context suggested means that sourcing best practice is an everyday activity, and that the power of reflection is fully understood.

Laughter, humour, and a sense of fun are quick to surface. A team that lacks humour, ongoing banter and, as appropriate, a sense of fun is missing the means to reduce tension, let the hot air out of inflated egos, or to build rapport between very different personalities.

Asking overwhelms telling. People are 80% more likely to buy in when they understand the reason behind the strategy or suggested change. In similar vein, they are far more likely to be committed to the change when they are fully involved in the process. And, as every parent of a teenager knows, collaboration presented as a request or suggestion has far more chance of succeeding than if delivered as an ultimatum.

Building trust never stops. Interpersonal trust is a very fragile commodity. It takes time to develop, but it can be quickly fractured. Personal trust is apparent when team members (a) deliver on **T**he promise, (b) show **R**espect for each other, (c) work to **U**nderstand the other person's point of view, (d) operate from a set of **S**hared values, and (e) **T**hrow away the mask of infallibility and deal with each other openly and honestly.

Ordinary folk are inspired to become heroes or heroines. When you hobble people's dreams you limit both their capacity and their willingness to reach out to others.

Respect is woven into the very fabric of everything the team does.

Accepting risk and pushing the boundaries is the default option. People push into new territory when they feel self-confident. Self-confidence, in turn, is an outcome of successfully overcoming risk. When people are fearful of making mistakes, barriers go up. When people are confronted with walls they cannot see beyond, they quickly settle for what is. When the "What's broken?" overrides the "What can we build on?" people see collaboration not as a way to grow, but as a burden that unnecessarily complicates their lives.

---

108 So-called "skunkworks" are but one example of this (see **Chapter one**, note 19). In some senses, what is being described is the business equivalent of a village green.

Technology is used in such a way that it both enables and simplifies connectivity. Here one needs to factor in all of the collaboration-enabling tools that Don Tapscott and Anthony D. Williams capture under their term "Wikinomics."[109] Peer-to-peer collaboration; co-creation of new products with partners, suppliers, and customers; and opening innovation to mass input have, literally, redefined traditional notions of "collaboration." When you move from "we" to "us," nothing stays the same.

Employee engagement is a business priority. People who do work that is mismatched with their capability have little interest in reaching out to support or engage their peers.

Collaboration is important within the team (intra-team). It is no less important between teams (inter-team). Although it means focusing on both the elements in the performance double helix and the **COLLABORATE** enablers outlined above, inter-team success demands even greater diligence when applying the behavioural glue that bonds together what are often unlike groups of people:

1. Team members need to get to know each other as individuals first.

2. Differences in culture, history, language, metaphor, the technology available, symbolism, and speed of action have to be surfaced early. The challenge is not to pull two (or more) teams together but to, in essence, create a third team that builds on the strengths of both. Create, not integrate!

3. The common purpose must be agreed upon by both teams.

4. When other priorites beckon, when resources are stretched, and when time is of the essence, the right leadership touch is essential.

5. In that formal power gives way to influence-power, intimidation, unreasonable demands, and threat destroy even the most resilient team alliances. Transparency, respect, trust, and a spirit of affirmation thus become the table stakes needed just to get into the game. Creative tension works; coercion doesn't. The golden rule: *No Surprises!*

6. There is no room for anything less than total agreement around goals, roles, and responsibilities. It is helpful to skew the reward system such that inter-team success is rewarded.

---

109 *Wikinomics: How Mass Collaboration Changes Everything* (Portfolio, 2008).

7. Conflict or inter-team rivalry must be addressed quickly and firmly. To that end, being forthright is a must from day one. Agree upon the team protocols early.

More communication isn't better communication, and the access to wider and faster networks doesn't necessarily mean more effective use of time and resources. Connectivity and, with it, the capacity for networking are gifts that science has bestowed on society in a new century. We must exploit this bequest, develop it, and recognize its value in building community, but we must also never forget who we are or how we got here as a species. Or, to quote President Gerald Ford, "Things are more like they are now than they have ever been."[110]

> *More communication isn't better communication.*

If you are the team leader: Know that, for collaboration to thrive, it has to be supported, as needed, by across-the-table dialogue: "Where are you really coming from?" "Can I trust you?" and candour-enabling, story-sharing, values-driven, humour-enriched, one-on-one, real-time conversations. Know that collaboration without trust is like trying to make bread without flour.

Do team members coach each other?

Outstanding teams – teams that flourish, blossom, and deliver – see learning and growth as a fundamental part of their makeup. A member of a great team, in turn, is an outstanding coach and, what is no less important, open to being coached. In a nimble and fast-moving team, team members coach each other. Always!

Coaching draws on seven qualities:

1. An optimistic view of tomorrow's possibility.

2. A deep-rooted belief that others on the team are ready, resourceful, and open to being coached.

3. A willingness to suspend assumptions about "the right way forward."

4. A recognition that giving advice isn't coaching.

5. Asking questions that enable those being coached to find their own path.

6. The capacity to listen, really listen.

7. Being supportive and affirming when the new behaviour emerges.

---

110 A quote also attributed to Dwight D. Eisenhower.

If you are the team leader: Coaching starts with you. If you don't coach, little intra- or cross-team coaching will take place. If you don't coach, one of the most effective performance improvement tools the team potentially has available is taken off the table. Know that coaching and trust are but different sides of the same coin; without one, the other cannot thrive.

Does the team take time out to celebrate success?

An old Egyptian proverb suggests, in essence, that "all work and no play make Jack a dull boy."[111] Teams that excel take time out to celebrate success. In coming out to play, the team allows the uniqueness of every team member to come through. In stepping outside of the day-to-day, they enable a different conversation. In slowing down and taking the time to reflect, they draw insight from recent events. In focusing on what worked, they make it more likely that the same behaviour will occur in the future. In creating space for celebration, they emphasize the power of results over the inadequacy of good intentions. Celebrating success starts to turn winning into a habit.

> *Celebrating success starts to turn winning into a habit.*

The team has to believe in the leader. More important still is that the leader believes in the team. Failure to take time out to celebrate success is a not-so-subtle message that the leader doesn't care; that the team's purpose is seen as subordinate to personal success; and that striving to avoid failure is more important than sharing the dream.

If you are the team leader: Know that meaning is the greatest motivator of all. Strive to find ways to improve the sightlines between the work people do and how that contribution makes a positive difference in people's lives. Know that if any of the building blocks of trust come under attack, yesterday's success all too easily becomes tomorrow's battlefield.

Is the capacity for renewal/reinvention part of the team's makeup?

Outstanding teams are driven by the belief that past solutions point the way to being tomorrow's runner-up and that to survive, let alone thrive, means to constantly challenge the way we do things. They are wired to understand that today's winning value proposition is tomorrow's commodity. As a result, outstanding teams constantly revisit both their aspirations and the way in which they work together as a team.

---

111 According to Wikipedia, the sentiment expressed by this proverb was first recorded by the Egyptian sage Ptahhotep, in 2400 BC.

Even the most expensive champagne goes flat. Stretch an elastic band for an extended period of time and it loses its "snap." Teams, including great teams, have a shelf life. Even the best get trapped by the established patterns of play. They start to recycle what worked yesterday.

When people start to get too comfortable with each other, the sharp corners get knocked off. The dilemma: Sustained performance success and complacency don't ride on the same bus. Creative tension needs an edge!

It happens in sport all the time. Championship-winning teams stay together too long. Paradoxically, the time to change is not when decline becomes apparent, but when the team is flying high, when the energy and momentum are at their peak. It takes a special kind of leader to change what is working. It takes courage to ask for a new deck; to reinvent what others admire; to hear the applause one minute and, in the very next, start the journey all over again. It takes tenacity, when the praise is being laid on thick, to draw the team together and start a discussion with the statement, "We need to revisit why we are here."

If you are the team leader: Write Andy Grove's guiding beliefs in the front of your diary: "Success breeds complacency. Complacency breeds failure. Only the paranoid survive."[112] Understand that knowing when to change is more important than knowing how to change. Know that if trust is lacking, change gets no backing.

Are three people a team?

Amongst all the talk about teams, a question that often arises is, "If there are only two or three of us – are we a team?" Well, if you were making the final push to the top of Everest, you would be a team. If you were playing four-ball[113] in a golf tournament you would be a team. And, yes, in a business environment, you and your colleagues are very much a team!

The double helix already outlined still applies, of course. The essence of building a great (small) team is still very much about a focus on both outcomes and relationships. So far so good, but leading a small team carries its own special challenges and rewards:

Coaching is the key to team success. It's important to tap into the potential of any team. When there are only two or three people, one middle-of-the-road performer is likely to set the standard of performance for the whole team. Set the bar high. Don't duck the tough conversation. Make coaching a way of life. Don't make the mistake of carrying a mediocre performer just because you can.

---

112 Andrew S. Grove became CEO of Intel in 1979 and chairman in 1997.

113 A golf game pitting two teams of two players (a total of four balls being played) against each other using "better-ball" scoring.

Hire the best. The smaller the team, the greater the damage wrought by a poor hire.

Efficiency shouldn't be confused with effectiveness. Because the span of control is small, because unbundling how the work of each team member creates value is relatively easy to do, reworking the key processes and striving to simplify everything the team does can, and should, become an overriding discipline.

Manage the boundaries. It's easy when you work closely with people to blur the line between being a colleague/friend and being the manager. There are times when you have to be the manager. There are times when the formal authority that goes with being a manager has to be exercised. Be caring, be respectful, but know that being overfamiliar will at first confuse but, before too long, destroy the trust of others on the team. A dilemma for any new manager, it can be especially problematic for a team member who is promoted to the manager role.

Invest in actions that build a sense of pride in everything the team does. It's often the case that a small team delivers year-in, year-out without being noticed. They can be, and often are, taken for granted. Strive to be the best team in the organization. Celebrate success. Make a mark. Push the boundaries. Make winning fun.

Share and solicit best practice. Someone, somewhere is doing what you are doing and doing it better. Do what it takes to find out who they are. Pass the learning on.

Train everyone on the team to do each other's role. Do it because you can. Do it because it emphasizes the sense of team. Do it because illness or extended absence of one member can cripple a small team.

Rotate talent often. It's easy for people in a small team to become too settled. Move people between smaller teams often. Renew the challenge regularly.

Yesterday's success has to be replaced by a focus on tomorrow's possibility. The internal competition within a larger team, the sense of creative tension that naturally falls from having a range of different personalities sitting around the table is often (invariably) missing from a small team. The result: Doing what we have always done in the way we have always done it, all too easily becomes the dominant mindset. Replace the conversation around who we are, and what we have achieved, with what we will become.

*If you are the team leader: Know that it's intent and generosity of spirit, not the number of people on the team that influences the nature and degree of trust. Know also that without trust, there will be plenty of **work** – but no **team.***

―――

Being the best can never be an outcome of striving to be merely good at something. Great organizations are built on great teams. Greatness doesn't happen by accident. It is enacted by leaders who build followership, who inspire, who are committed to win, who are quick to act, who surround themselves with high performers, and who know how to forge that same group into an outstanding team.

Leaders who deliver team excellence see the team not as a series of problems to be solved, but as an orchard to be tended. They move beyond a mechanistic view of the world. They influence team performance, not by changing parts of the system, but working the system as a whole. They act from the belief that redefining possibility lies, in the first instance, in managing the context.

This is not to suggest that poor performance should be tolerated or that individuals who lack anything less than 100% commitment should be allowed to remain part of the team. What it does portray is that the right leader, before making any decisions about individuals on the team, will always ask, "Am I the right leader? To what extent am I part of the problem? Does the team have a compelling purpose? Is the strategy clear? Are the roles and expectations unambiguously defined? Does everyone on the team understand how they can enrich the team overall? Is straight talk part of how everyone on the team thinks and acts? Are the means to collaborate in place? Do we coach each other? Do we have an ethos of affirmation and do we celebrate success? Is the challenge on hand to continue to strive to become better at what we have always done, or is to revisit what we really mean when we use the word 'team'?"

> *A leader who acts precipitously, who attempts to fix the cracks without examining the vessel is displaying behaviour that, at root, lacks integrity.*

A leader who acts precipitously, who attempts to fix the cracks without examining the vessel is displaying behaviour that, at root, lacks integrity. That does not mean that the questions drawn out of the performance double helix are tabled only when the team has encountered troubled water. The marketplace, customers' needs, and the expectations of employees are destined to change whether we want them to or not – often in unexpected ways.

The organization's emerging culture is central to how the organization competes tomorrow. Arguably, it is the only thing the organization has that the competition cannot easily recreate. The team is the basic building block of that culture. Leaders who succeed, leaders who care, leaders who are driven to make a difference constantly revisit one truly profound question: "What do I have to do to take the team to the next level?"

Next steps

To what extent have the following criteria of team success been realised?

		Hardly at all				Somewhat			Absolutely		
1.	Compelling purpose	1	2	3	4	5	6	7	8	9	10
2.	The right leader	1	2	3	4	5	6	7	8	9	10
3.	The right strategy	1	2	3	4	5	6	7	8	9	10
4.	The right people	1	2	3	4	5	6	7	8	9	10
5.	Functional roles clear	1	2	3	4	5	6	7	8	9	10
6.	Team roles clear	1	2	3	4	5	6	7	8	9	10
7.	Goals clear	1	2	3	4	5	6	7	8	9	10
8.	Protocols agreed	1	2	3	4	5	6	7	8	9	10
9.	Candour	1	2	3	4	5	6	7	8	9	10
10.	Collaboration	1	2	3	4	5	6	7	8	9	10
11.	Coach each other	1	2	3	4	5	6	7	8	9	10
12.	Celebration	1	2	3	4	5	6	7	8	9	10
13.	Renewal as needed	1	2	3	4	5	6	7	8	9	10

If leaders across the organization were to successfully take their team to the next level, we would:

_____

_____

_____

_____

_____

_____

_____

As an organization, to build great teams – regardless of level or location – we need to:

_____

_____

_____

_____

_____

_____

_____

_____

Starting now, to take my own team to the next level, I commit to:

_____

_____

_____

_____

_____

_____

_____

_____

Chapter six:
IF YOU CAN'T COACH, YOU CAN'T LEAD!

In an upside-down world

Yesterday's leadership was about the power derived from authority and knowledge. When everything else was stripped away, it was about control. It was about being, and always appearing to be, the boss. Savvy leaders today realise that today's leadership has "influence" written all over it. They know that, even if they wanted to, they can no longer do it on their own. They understand that, as a leader, they can't **not** coach. They appreciate that when finding and retaining good people is becoming ever-more difficult, growing and developing that talent isn't an option. They work from the belief that their own career progression rests on their ability to mobilize the human potential on the team.

The narrative of a trapped mind

"I really don't have time to coach."

"To be honest, although we talk a lot about the need to coach, the environment doesn't support coaching."

"If my boss knew how to coach, I know I would be a better and more enthusiastic coach."

"I have been trained how to solve problems. It's how I am made. Every time I get it in my mind that this is a coaching opportunity, I feel compelled to 'give the answer.'"

"The only thanks you get for being a great coach is that you become a source of talent for colleagues who don't coach."

The rest of the story …

Mastery is effortless delivery without thinking.

If you can't coach, you can't lead!

"Coaching is all about challenging the motivated and not motivating the challenged."

Gone is a time when one strong man or woman could brave the maelstrom alone. Gone is a time where titular power, ego, privilege, prestige, and self-promotion provided the agenda for followership. And past is the era when knowing the answer was deemed to be more important than the quality of the questions asked.

Enter the new facts of business life: a need to build community – and with it, shared accountability, collaboration, openness, diversity, and the recognition that those who worship at the altar of command-and-control are following a false prophet. Giving life to these emerging leadership imperatives, finally bursting forth into full bloom, is **coaching.**

Coaching describes a systemic leadership approach – not simply a set of new skills or a cloak to be tossed aside when the **real** work needs to be done. Being a great coach starts by stepping down from the stage; it implies being able to see the world through the eyes of those who are being asked to follow; it builds on a simple assumption that "given the chance, people will get it right."

As a leader, you can't **not** coach. Praise is coaching. Ignoring the tough conversation is coaching. Travelling first-class when the service rep who fixes the machines you sell sits at the back of the plane is coaching. Keeping people waiting is coaching. How you start a meeting is coaching. Listening is coaching. Asking questions is coaching. Encouraging and responding to suggestions is coaching. Candour, or the lack of it, is coaching. As a leader you do a whole lot of coaching – even if much of it you are unaware of. The problem: Spending time on something doesn't necessarily make you good at it. The dilemma: *If you can't coach, you can't lead!*

What follows are **3 x 7** suggestions about how to make coaching central to how you lead. Step one: The 7 building blocks of a coaching culture. Step two: The 7 coaching disciplines. Step three: The 7 imperatives that frame a successful coaching conversation.

Step one: The 7 building blocks of a coaching culture

"The act of coaching is, in no small measure, about helping the coachee understand how to win."

In examining how leading organizations create a coaching culture, what one finds is that the bedrock of their success lies in a common belief system – a collective ethos about the role of coaching in ongoing business success. Coaching is not an activity. It's a "way to be" enabled by organizational and emotional architecture encompassing the following:

1. **Water doesn't flow uphill, and coaching cannot thrive unless the business environment supports it.** Here five questions, in particular, are pivotal: (1) Is there genuine clarity around the culture the organization is seeking to create?[114] (2) Do the organization's leadership competencies directly support coaching as a critical leadership capability? (3) Does the compensation system reward managers for growing talent? (4) Do leaders at the top exhibit coaching mastery? (5) Are those in key leadership roles open to be coached? If the answer to any one of these questions is "no," "maybe," or "sometimes" and you want to embed coaching as a core discipline, you have work to do.

2. **A system can never be stronger than its weakest link.** Coaching is an integral part of a successful talent management system. By way of example, unless leaders bring coaching excellence to the table, the investment in performance management, 360° feedback, employee engagement, leadership development, succession planning, and leadership integration is largely for naught. That talent management is truly a system can be seen in the reality that a good deal of what is sometimes referred to as "remedial coaching" is little more than an attempt to address a poor hiring decision.

3. **Coaching is all about challenging the motivated and not motivating the challenged.** The act of coaching is about enabling the coachee to understand how to win. Coaching, at its best, is thus all about building on strengths. Here it is important to differentiate between:

   > *Counselling:* addressing problems and issues where the underlying causation lies outside of the workplace.

---

114 Coaching that fails to factor in the "emerging culture" is a mandate to do more – albeit better – of what we have always done.

> *Mentoring:* a seasoned performer who shares their story with a less seasoned performer, the outcome being that the latter is accelerated through the learning curve.

> *Training:* new skills.

> *Teaching:* new knowledge.

> *Coaching:* a performance-based conversation drawn out of a serving spirit. At its best, it is centred around hard questions, a soft voice, listening ears, and a tough-minded attitude about the need to act. [115]

4. **There are four distinctly different approaches to coaching.** Figure six outlines those approaches while, at the same time, describing the conditions needed to ensure that each flourishes. Although rooted in dialogue, coaching is about far more than just the "conversation." As suggested, it sits at the very centre of a successful talent management system:

   1. *Performance coaching:* taking the employee to the next level in the current role. Performance coaching supports and is integral to a meaningful performance management process.

   2. *Development coaching:* supporting and developing the employee to the point of being ready to move into a bigger or broader role. Development coaching lies at the centre of a successful succession agenda.

   3. *In-the-moment coaching:* opportunist and often "accidental." Leadership is ultimately about the quality of the conversations that take place every day. The richest form of in-the-moment coaching is reinforcing early success.

   4. *Coaching in how to coach:* someone who is not only an outstanding coach but who can share with others the basis for that success. If you have people like this in your organization, make sure they do not join the competition.

5. **Helping people doesn't help.** Paradoxically, leaders who see coaching as "helping" – as opposed to guiding or empowering – are not really helping the employee. This is not to decry the need for leaders to care. The dilemma: using a term from an old Harvard Business Review article, in the desire to "help," a myriad

---

115 Taken from *Myth, Magic, Mindset* (2008).

Building a Coaching Culture

Approach \ Activity	Performance coaching	Developmental coaching	In-the-Moment coaching	Coaching in how to coach
Approach	Enhanced performance in current role. By implication, poor performance isn't tolerated	Building capability to succeed in a larger role. This also assumes excellence in talent acquisition	Highly skilled response to unexpected coaching opportunity	Masterful coaching is both recognized and rewarded
	1 2 3 4 5 6 7 8 9 10	1 2 3 4 5 6 7 8 9 10	1 2 3 4 5 6 7 8 9 10	1 2 3 4 5 6 7 8 9 10
Draws on	A performance management system that gives equal weight to (1) results and (2) competencies (or values)	A succession process anchored in "tomorrow's" culture. This means we "measure" culture	A spirit of affirmation across the organization	A coaching ethos clearly evident at the very top of the organization
	1 2 3 4 5 6 7 8 9 10	1 2 3 4 5 6 7 8 9 10	1 2 3 4 5 6 7 8 9 10	1 2 3 4 5 6 7 8 9 10
Demands	A willingness on the part of the coach to let go of wanting to "solve the problem"	"Testing" the employee against the role-specific competencies demanded before being moved into a new role	An environment where employees are encouraged to take risk	Established coaching protocols applied consistently throughout the organization
	1 2 3 4 5 6 7 8 9 10	1 2 3 4 5 6 7 8 9 10	1 2 3 4 5 6 7 8 9 10	1 2 3 4 5 6 7 8 9 10

Figure six

of leaders have fallen into the trap of collecting "monkeys" that rightfully belong to the employee.[116]

For example, when a team member walks into your office with a question, the vast majority of the time they **already** know the answer. Providing the answer doesn't help! Coaching is a partnership, but one where ownership of the agreed outcome rests with the coachee. When the coachee outlines the "where to from here," learning and growth come to the fore. Creating the space for the employee to act also enables the manager to escape from "doing" and spend more time "thinking." We love to help people. A helping mentality, however, comes at a cost: time set aside to make sure those same problems don't occur in the first place. Managers who do both their own work and much of the decision making one-level-down

---

116 William Oncken and Donald Wass, "Management Time: Who's Got the Monkey?" *Harvard Business Review,* (November-December,1974), pp 75–80.

may project the illusion of being busy, but by no stretch of the imagination should they delude themselves into thinking that they are being effective. *Stop collecting monkeys!*

> *The best return on investment comes from coaching high-potential employees.*

6. Not every conversation should, or needs to be, a coaching conversation. Good coaches pick their spots. Mastery is to know **when** and **who** to coach. Identifying the coaching moment is a matter of judgment and experience. How to coach is a function of knowing *who to challenge, who to coach, who to confront, and who to change.* (See Figure seven.)[117] The best return on investment comes from coaching high-potential employees. Top performers who feel they're not being challenged and/or stretched are about to join an organization that **will** challenge them. All well and good, you might say, but when everyone in today's organization is attempting to do more with less, how do successful leaders ever find the time to coach?

One rather cryptic answer is that if you don't coach, what you **will** have is plenty of time. A more pragmatic response is that the only way to find more time to coach – is to coach.

Doesn't live the values ... delivers results	Lives the values ... delivers results
CONFRONT (Live our values or work elsewhere)	**CHALLENGE** (Developmental coaching)
Who to coach?	
CHANGE (Move out)	**COACH** (Performance coaching)
Doesn't live the values ... doesn't deliver results	Lives the values ... doesn't deliver results

Figure seven

---

117 Draws on the GE performance grid.

7. **Coaching the individual is a subset of coaching the team.** We are team animals. *Homo sapiens* literally survived because of our ability to work together. Accordingly, great organizations are built on great teams. Beliefs, performance standards, willingness to take risk, propensity for openness, the spirit of sharing (collaboration), and challenging the way things have always been done, are all heavily influenced by the team. In a similar vein, it's tough for the coachee to enter fully into the coaching conversation if there is ambiguity around the role; if the objectives for both the team and each team member are unclear; or where there is confusion around individual accountability and responsibility. Coaching the individual and, at the same time, largely ignoring the influence of the team is a little like riding the lift to the top of the snow-covered mountain, looking down and finding you only have one ski. It should also be emphasized that coaching is not the exclusive prerogative of the team leader. In a great team, team members coach each other. Peer coaching may, indeed, be the most impactful coaching of all!

If the business context doesn't support successful coaching, investment in "coaching skills" amounts to pursuit of a lost cause. Coaching cannot flourish in a vacuum. No less important, if a coaching mindset isn't fully present in the organization's leadership point of view, a whole lot of other key processes – starting with performance management – will be found wanting.

Step two: The 7 coaching disciplines

"A great question changes the conversation the coachee is having with him/herself."

Mastery is a process whereby knowledge expertise and insight move from being a series of conscious actions to the point where they become an intuitive and natural part of one's behaviour. Mastery is effortless delivery without thinking. It's the impression given to others that the greater the crisis, the greater the calm. It's the appearance of always having extra time. And the source of mastery? It's clearly about practice, practice, and then more practice. It's about a passion to excel. It's about clarity of purpose. It's about focus. And it's about a desire to be the best. Beyond anything mentioned, however, mastery is a discipline! A discipline rooted in a series of simple truths and ingrained routines. Positive habits that, from a coaching perspective, embrace the following:

1. **Cheering works!** A successful coach is skilled in the way he/she contracts for the coaching conversation. From the first moment, elegant and effective rapport can be assumed. The setting and timing are well chosen. Interruptions aren't tolerated. And, of course, the coach has done the homework. All that counts for naught, however, if "coaching" is perceived as the inevitable "reward" for less than stellar performance. In a business environment where "gotcha" is the norm, even the hint that the manager wants to have a coaching conversation is likely to induce an employee reaction along the lines of "What have I done wrong now?" By comparison, optimism and a spirit of affirmation set the scene such that, rather than being viewed as an invitation to climb the gallows, even the toughest coaching conversation is underscored by positive intent.

2. **What the coach believes is what the coachee perceives.** Over 90% of what we communicate happens at a non-conscious level. If the coach doesn't believe that the actions being charted by the coachee are within the coachee's capability – even if the coach remains silent – that belief will have a profound impact on the eventual outcome. To coach is to believe. And if you don't believe? You've got to believe! A masterful coach projects a deep and residing belief that the coachee **will** (not might, not could) deliver the change being discussed.

3. **An experienced coach comes to the conversation with a beginner's mind.** Those trapped by past "expertise" and a need to be right invariably have the solution (the coach's solution, that is) mapped out as soon as the issue is surfaced. In doing so, they strangle creativity and limit possibility. To work from a beginner's mind is to be open to being surprised; it is to pick up and follow a direction being charted that the coach would not have anticipated. A beginner's mind affirms possibility and encourages risk. It opens the door for the coach to be a full participant in the learning experience. If you even flirt with the notion of being superior or, in any way, better than the person sitting opposite you, not only can't you coach, but you won't learn.

4. **Beyond problem solving.** There are a number of meaningful conversations that take place at the workplace. Three in particular punctuate even the busiest manager's day: (1) tell-and-listen – "I want you to ..." (2) tell-and-sell – "I want you to because ..." and (3) problem solving – "Why don't you and I sit down

and between us figure out the best solution?" These are perfectly legitimate conversations, but they are not about coaching.

Coaching is an advice-free zone. When the manager comes up with suggestions or says, "Have you thought of ..." or "my idea is ...," it may be a great interjection, but it isn't coaching. Tell-and-listen and tell-and-sell conversations are all about "power over." Problem solving is "power with." Coaching is "power to." And the difference is important.

The world we have entered demands new thinking around the use and distribution of power at the workplace: leadership of the context. Agility, innovation, speed, and responsiveness evolve only where the dominant mindset encourages risk. Mastery in coaching is to move beyond problem solving.

5. **To coach is to ask great questions.** A great question changes the conversation the coachee is having with him/ herself. It asks for what is wanted, and doesn't reinforce what isn't wanted. "Describe what success would look like" is to ask for what is wanted. "Tell me what is holding you back" reinforces what isn't wanted. Great questions come not from preparation but from, paradoxically, not knowing. When we allow the question to simply bubble up from our non-conscious mind, we are tapping into that part of our make-up often referred to as "wisdom." When we move from "the head" and start to engage our intuition and experience, when we stop trying to control the conversation and start being in the conversation, a simpler, more grounded conversation surfaces. Keeping it simple is found in short, succinct, non-directive questions, the masterful use of silence, and an ability to uncover and build on ways in which the coachee is already successful.

> *A great question changes the conversation the coachee is having with him/ herself.*

6. **To coach is to listen, really listen.** We listen when we put the needs of others ahead of our own needs; when we put a hold on likely interruptions; when we clear the clutter from our mind. We listen when we hear what isn't being said; when we are conscious of the subtext behind the message; and when the tone, pace, and projection of the language reveals what the coachee is conflicted about – or seeking to move towards. Listening clearly involves the ears, but it starts in the

body. We listen when we slow down, when we inhale deeply, when we relax the muscles in our lower jaw, and when we find that inner core of quiet that lies inside all of us. Listening isn't a spectator sport. Listening is hard work. And guess what! When we listen to others, we start listening to ourselves. Coaching mastery is about listening to others in the way you have always wanted to be listened to.

> *If the outcome of the coaching conversation isn't written down, it won't happen.*

7. Pass ownership to the coachee. If you have teenage children, you are only too aware that agreeing to what needs to be done is a far cry from it actually getting done. A successful coaching session has a strong ending: who is going to do what and when. Agreed goals must be specific. They should be both short-term (immediately, tomorrow, next week), and longer-term. Timelines are essential. The language the coachee uses – both verbal and in the body – should convey to the coach, "I will make it happen." Feedback that suggests, "I will give it my best shot," "I will work on that," or "I will certainly try" signal that the agreed goals are subject to the whims of fate.

If the outcome of the coaching conversation isn't written down, it won't happen. Who should write it down? The coachee. Who is responsible for follow up? In the first instance, the coachee. Where the coachee fails to keep the coach informed, the latter must act. Coaching without follow-up is to do the work, send the invoice, and then not cash the cheque.

Step three: The 7 imperatives that frame a successful coaching conversation

"The coaching conversation is a strand of cultural DNA that contains within it the blueprint for (1) managing expectations and (2) building self-confidence."

There are numerous qualities associated with being a great coach. **One** is non-negotiable: humility. Trust, respect, and rapport – essential elements of the coaching conversation – all fall by the wayside if inflated ego, the need for control, political expediency, or an attitude of "I know best" frame the conversation. Coaching is never about the coach. Without humility, no amount of training can transform a self-focused manager into a good coach.

No less damaging is when what the coach **says** is misaligned with what the coach **does.**

Humility represents the centre of gravity for any positive coaching experience. Without it, silent manoeuvring and resentment lead inevitably to defensiveness and emotional flight. Without humility, coercion soon enters the fray. Without humility, going deep lies outside any sense of the possible. Humility transforms coaching into a learning opportunity for those involved. Humility is the breath of possibility that enables change to take flight. Humility is the emotional anchor that enables the seven imperatives of a winning coaching conversation to hold fast:

1. **Being there.** Although a number of techniques and tools can help improve coaching effectiveness, mastery is ultimately about "how the coach turns up." Setting aside judgment, building rapport, being open to be surprised and adopting a serving mindset far outweigh any specific technique. To coach is to cast aside the mask; not to assume; not to reflect; not to analyze; simply, to be in the moment and to be there – **really** be there.

2. **A "map" helps.** Coaching benefits when the coach is able to navigate a way through the conversation; when the coach knows exactly where in the discussion he/she is. This speaks to a series of conversational building blocks that, like a jigsaw puzzle, **can be put down in any order,** but in which every piece is needed for the picture to be complete.[118] These building blocks are as follows:

> *What is the issue/opportunity?* Dig to uncover the underlying issue.

> *What does future success look like?* Move the coachee into "tomorrow" and have him/her create "the success video."

> *What is happening today?* Challenge, seek the truth, be honest. Validate past success. "Scale" the current reality: If the "video" is a "10," calibrate where we are today. Move beyond **who's** right – uncover **what's** right.

> *To coach is to cast aside the mask; not to assume; not to reflect; not to analyze; simply, to be in the moment and to be there – really be there.*

118 If the term "model" outlines a series of linear, predetermined, and sequential steps, we have found little evidence to support the value of a coaching model. How and where an experienced coach enters into the coaching conversation depends on the challenge at hand, and it is drawn out of the relationship the coach already has (or doesn't have) with the coachee.

> *What is the one change that, were it to happen, would make the greatest difference?* Focus on one thing at a time. As appropriate, draw out new knowledge, new ideas, new thinking, new language, or best practice elsewhere. Explore different scenarios by asking: What feels right? What represents the simplest process? What actions play into the coachee's strengths? If the coachee is identified as a successor for a key role, what next steps would best test his/her capability? Seek ways to be affirming.

> > *Which specific, time-bounded, stretch goals describe tomorrow's success?* Push for action. Agree on the resources needed. Test for commitment. Identify potential, unintended consequences. Make sure the coachee understands the significance and impact – business and personal – of failing to meet the agreed outcomes. Work agreed goals into the scorecard.

> > *How will we know that success has been achieved?* Agree on milestones. Follow up. Look for opportunities to reinforce success. Emphasize that the coachee is responsible for keeping you fully informed.

> Where to begin? Depending on the relationship and the situation, the coaching conversation can start with 360° feedback, by drawing out the real issue through a robust discussion around today's reality, by agreeing on what success with a specific customer needs to look like, or, indeed, by either the coach or coachee tabling the issue at the outset. Remember, you need all of the pieces to complete the picture, but based on the situation and the relationship, you can play them in any order.

> *A masterful coach knows the issue that comes up early in the coaching conversation is often not the real issue.*

3. **The real issue is often hidden.** A masterful coach knows the issue that comes up early in the coaching conversation is often not the real issue. How to get to the latter? Use simple questions to dig deeper, such as "Tell me more" and "Go on." The more the coachee talks about "the issue," the more likely they are to peel the onion and get to the real issue. Silence is often the best question of all.

4. **Not every coaching conversation has to result in a home run.** The coaching conversation is a strand of cultural DNA that contains within it the blueprint for (1) managing expectations and (2) building self-confidence. Success means that, even with a high-potential employee, a successful outcome may, on occasion,

be no more than the coachee agreeing to pursue a specific idea or meeting with someone who can provide additional input. Like breaking up a log-jam, there are times when a small adjustment can make a big difference.

5. **Coaching isn't the soft option.** Coaching is often mistakenly framed as a soft option. To be a coach is to be a fact-seeker and a truth-teller. It is to be "tough-minded." Tough-minded enough to be candid when needed. Tough-minded enough to know that, although work–life balance is desirable and a supportive climate is needed, coaching is ultimately the pursuit of performance excellence. Tough-minded enough to step in at the earliest signs that performance is slipping. Tough-minded enough to act when the employee is behaving in a way that is misaligned with the organization's values. Tough-minded enough to ring the changes when it is clear that the employee is in the wrong role. Tough-minded enough to confront the individual concerned when the employee's agenda works against the success of others on the team.

6. **Not everyone is open to being coached.** Although some literature might suggest otherwise, not everyone is open to being coached. For instance, "Just tell me what to do! I am way too busy!"; lack of trust; concern about appearing vulnerable; ego issues ("Who is he to coach me!"); "Been there, done that ... and it didn't work!" and a host of other self-inflicted prejudices can serve to lock even potentially outstanding employees out of the coaching experience. It is naive in the extreme to assume that those who are not open to being coached will go on to become good coaches themselves. Clearly, it's a mistake to promote someone who isn't willing to be coached. Better still, don't hire that person in the first place.

> *Although some literature might suggest otherwise, not everyone is open to being coached.*

7. **Even the most talented people get stuck from time to time.** Coaching mastery moves into overdrive when the coachee is "stuck." Faced with that situation, the experienced coach explores a series of pivotal questions (see Figure eight):

   > *Is this a "can't do" or "won't do" dilemma?* If it's a "won't do" situation, to what extent am I part of the problem? Would moving the individual into a different role make sense?

> *If it's a "can't do" problem, would training or access to new knowledge make a difference?*

> *Is the coachee using self-defeating language or self-talk that prevents them from taking action?* Examples include self-fulfilling statements ("I will never be any good at ... "); deflection ("The real problem lies with ... "); being trapped by the past ("We have never done it that way"); confusing working hard with working smart ("I don't have the time right now"); or presenting personal perception/ beliefs as the unmitigated truth ("We will never be able to ... ").

> *What is working right now – even if occasionally – that we can build upon?* Quoting Bill Clinton, "Leadership is far more about the power of example than it is the example of power."[119]

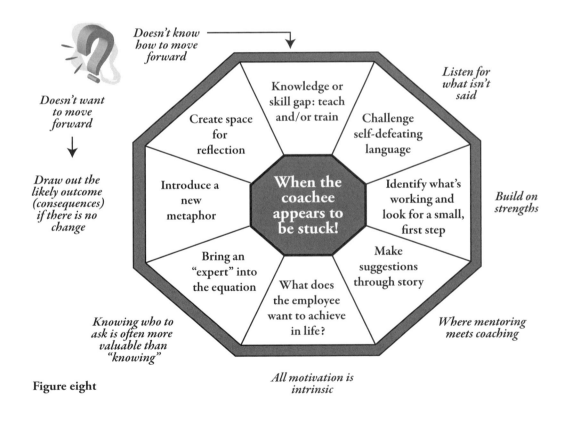

Figure eight

---

119 A term that originated in General Electric.

› *Would moving from a coaching into a mentoring role make a difference?* Mentoring is not just a kinder and gentler way to give advice. Mentoring is sharing experience. It provides structure whereby the coachee can explore potential next steps, understand what has worked elsewhere, and access learning that the mentor has had time to reflect on personally. Telling or giving advice is "power over." Sharing a story is "power to." The former is about control. Because the coachee can choose to accept the gift of the story or not, the latter passes ownership to the employee. Commitment, engagement, and growth ultimately lie with a "power to" relationship.

› *What does the employee want to achieve in life?* In what ways can that latent inner drive be brought to the challenge on hand? Like a water diviner, where others see a desert, the very best coaches uncover the source of energy and life.

› *Would there be value in bringing an "expert" into the equation?* The term "expert" here means either (1) a qualified and respected individual and/or (2) reaching out to explore best practice.

› *In that our intentions are shaped by imagery, which new metaphor, were it introduced into the conversation, would reframe how the coachee sees the world?* Like a great question, the right metaphor provides a compelling "picture" of the way forward (the boundaryless organization[120]). By way of comparison, a poorly thought-through metaphor – one that reinforces and makes more likely what you don't want – is a cultural virus that can do untold damage (let's get rid of the silos.)

› *Recognizing that people learn in different ways, will the individual in question benefit from reflecting on the issue for a few days?* In many instances, the answer is yes ... an emphatic "Yes!"

120 A term that originated in General Electric.

Goodnight, Mr. Earp!

Scene one: Profits are down, margins have been eroding, expenses are up, and a few months ago we made the decision to bring onboard a hard-nosed business person – an executive who would shake up the business.

Scene two: The individual we hired brings renewed focus to the business results, is assertive, sets tough goals, and holds people accountable. That take-charge approach appeared to be exactly what the organization needed! Indeed the CEO asked, "Why didn't we do this before?"

Scene three: The new executive is clearly talented, but recently it has started to become clear that this individual just doesn't seem to fit in. An unproductive tension has surfaced in the team; several key subordinates appear to be non-supportive; peers don't always hold the individual in very high esteem; and "the grapevine" has moved into full-destruct mode.

Why is this executive struggling? The need for leaders to gain buy-in, the essential role that candour plays in team success, and that Gen Y employees, in particular, bring a healthy level of cynicism to edicts and instructions (being told what to do) – all this has created a business climate where bringing in a "gunfighter" amounts to a lynching in the making. A leader whose behaviour would have been highly lauded in the immediate past is on a self-destruct path today.

Organizations have long held leaders in the Wyatt Earp mould in high esteem. The tough, charismatic, well-groomed, great-at-managing-up, problem-solver who, calculator already unholstered, rides slowly into town, armed with a single-minded attitude about the need to bring about change and a determination to lay down the law.

What this scenario ignores is that Tombstone has been renamed "Google"; the "Buntline Special" shot its last owner in the foot; and aggression that begets fear is about as good a way to prevent change as you can get. Organizations need tough-minded, assertive, bottom-line focused leaders, but not those trained in the "it's all about me" school of charm and deportment – and certainly not those who can't or won't coach.

As an organization, if all of those in key leadership roles – regardless of level – delivered mastery in coaching, we would:

_____

_____

_____

_____

_____

_____

_____

As an organization, to build a coaching culture we need to:

_____

_____

_____

_____

_____

_____

_____

Starting now, to take my own coaching capability to the next level, I will:

_____

_____

_____

_____

_____

_____

_____

Chapter seven:
THE TOUGH CONVERSATION

In an upside-down world

An education system that works to make sure students don't fail, a commercial marketplace that offers immediate gratification, and a shift in power from the organization to the employee have created a business climate where a sense of entitlement is becoming ever-more prevalent. Organizations have to be sensitive to the needs of the new workforce, but that response cannot be offered as a blank cheque. Leaders, regardless of their function or level, cannot afford to step back from the conversation that outlines, "This is what we demand of you." To that end, more then ever, to lead is to know how and when to deliver the tough conversation.

The narrative of a trapped mind

"When push comes to shove, when I hold people accountable, I all too often discover there is a lack of support (from above) for letting the individual go."

"We are inconsistent. It's difficult for me to hold a strong line around performance in my area when elsewhere it appears others get away with murder."

"It's difficult to challenge someone around values when our values are less than clear. It's also the case that several of those at the top seem to be less than 100% wedded to our values."

"Half of the people who report to me have been here forever. They do just enough to get by but display little or no sense of urgency. If I become tough-minded with any one them, they close ranks and, as a group, work to diminish my reputation in the business."

"The performance management process is skewed heavily towards the results achieved, such that the behaviour needed to support those results gets swamped by the plaudits and sense of satisfaction that go with 'getting the job done.'"

The rest of the story …

Not to act is to extend permission.

The tough conversation

"When you look up commitment in the dictionary, nowhere does it make reference to: 'I will do my best.'"

We've all been there: an otherwise successful subordinate whose performance is inconsistent; a direct report whose behaviour bumps up against the organization's values; someone on your team who, although an excellent individual contributor, is not a team player.

Leadership is about a lot of things. It's about being open to the unexpected. It's about protecting the core. It's about nurturing agility. It's about change. It's about creating the space for innovation to take hold. No less, it's about making hard decisions. It's about facing up to those all-too-easily-put-off difficult conversations – conversations that, if not managed effectively, can bruise a talented employee who happens to have wandered off-track, or can inflame an already difficult situation.

> *Not to act is to abdicate virtually everything it means to be a leader.*

In ducking the tough conversations, we are not simply pushing them to one side. Doing nothing is a form of action. Inaction extends permission. Holding back conveys the unmistakable message, "It's okay to continue doing what you are doing."

Leaders **must** lead! Not to act is to abdicate virtually everything it means to be a leader. And do not assume that performance reticence lies exclusively with inexperienced middle managers. Because the relationships are often long-founded and personal, top leaders are, if anything, the group most reluctant to face up to the tough conversation.

Essential as these conversations are in good times, when you are fighting for your organizational life, confronting performance shortfalls or problematic behaviour takes on added importance. In times like these, how we manage the beliefs and assumptions that shape the informal organization, how we manage the stories that fuel the "grapevine" determine what is possible. When one manager raises the bar or takes a tough performance stance, that "message" reverberates across the organization. When leaders act in concert, the "message" becomes an anthem that even the most skeptical employee will find impossible to ignore. Survival isn't about what the top team **wants** to do; it's about what those in the middle of the organization are **prepared** to do. It's about how they define "success."

There are any number of reasons why employees fail to deliver what has been agreed. Go through the 10-point checklist below before having the tough conversation:

(1) Are the goals clear?

(2) Does the employee know how to do what needs to be done?

(3) Has he/she disagreed with you in the past about the worth of doing what was agreed?

(4) Have other priorities entered the equation?

(5) Are there positive outcomes for being successful?

(6) Are there clear consequences for failing?

(7) Am I part of the problem? Is there a conflict between the demands of the different matrixed reporting relationships?

(8) Are there barriers or obstacles outside the employee's control?

(9) Are external factors (e.g., health, family issues) getting in the way?

(10) Is the position a "widow maker?" Have others failed in this role?

We want people to like us. Conflict is uncomfortable: "I know I **should** have the conversation, but things seem to be getting a little better." "While it's true that little has improved, perhaps I'm expecting too much from him." "Sometimes key targets are missed, but she is extremely popular with everyone else on the team."

When the outer veneer of ambivalence is stripped away, managers are deeply aware that if they don't act, the current situation will prevail. They hold back, for the most part, because they don't know **how** to have the tough conversation.

What follows are ideas and suggestions around the two central issues in the tough conversation. Part one looks at setting the context. Part two explores **how** to move through the conversation.

Part one: The context

The tough conversation we are describing doesn't exist in a vacuum. We stumble when pieces of the puzzle are missing, when leadership is absent, when the conversation comes as a surprise, when a sense of entitlement swamps the "unrelenting drive to deliver" embedded in the word "commitment." When you look up *commitment* in the dictionary, **nowhere** does it make reference to: "I will do my best."

> *Leadership is an act of service.*

If "context" is found in the emotional intent that lies behind the language we use, it is no less about how the act of leadership unfolds. Leadership is an act of service. When everything else is stripped away, it's about bringing the best out in others. It's also a discipline – a code of behaviour that has to be practised each and every day. A leader delivers that discipline when he/she:

> Brings clarity to the direction being charted.

> Clarifies and personally lives the organization's values.

> Makes meeting the agreed targets an unremitting "mantra" – a palpable beat that plays in the background of every meeting, every conversation, and every presentation.

> Builds an environment of trust based on the belief that people want to be successful, want to make a difference, and want to be fully engaged by the work they do.

> Ensures that everyone on the team understands their role and the responsibilities and accountabilities framed by that role.

> Gains commitment to the key outcomes (ideally, a scorecard for the role) from everyone on the team and holds those same individuals accountable.

> Identifies the specific behavioural competencies for each role.

> Encourages "straight talk."

> Makes coaching a way of life.

> Acts fast if unwarranted behaviour or performance slippage becomes apparent.

> Develops a reputation for being both consistent and fair.

> Makes feedback – especially positive feedback – a way of life.

Like streams flowing into a river, these leadership disciplines converge to shape a business environment where the tough conversation, far from being an emotional aberration, is simply a natural part of how people work together.

The caution here is that each leadership "tributary" is important; each, if not enacted, can poison the wider waterway (context). By way of example: If little trust is displayed, the leader will not be heard; if the goals are ambiguous, accountability is an irrelevant concept; if honesty is missing, a hidden agenda can be assumed; if coaching is a sometime event, growth and challenge have little currency; and if the leader's role in life is largely to comment on what **isn't** working, the assumption that there will be a receptive ear to yet one more criticism is a form of optimism that shares much with a mindset that prompts people to buy a lottery ticket.

Here, a word about "the team." Little, if anything, influences the individual's behaviour as strongly as do the attitude, norms, and performance ethos of others on the team. A great team carries no passengers. The peer pressure exerted by a high-performance team has far more impact than **any** form of censure (including potential termination) provided by the formal leader. Strong and sustained individual performance is enabled by a strong team. Overcoming unanticipated hurdles depends on the support of a strong team. Learning and growth is enriched by a strong team. The principles at work here are these: (1) Great teams both drive and support outstanding individual performance, and (2) The overall performance of a marginal team will inevitably and inextricably be shaped (often sooner rather than later) by the weakest link. Great teams are self-regulating. Struggling teams invariably embrace the lowest common denominator.

"Performance" is a word that is bandied around a good deal. What does it really mean? Sir John Whitmore, the British coaching guru, describes performance in the following terms: "Real performance is going beyond what is expected; it is setting one's own highest standards, invariably standards that surpass what others demand or expect."[121] Here one needs to add that "performance" encompasses, without exception, both **what** was achieved (results) and **how** it was achieved (behaviour).

There is one more issue to cover: building on success. No matter what the endeavour, champions climb onto the podium because they have an intimate relationship with what it is that makes them strong. No leader made it to the top because they displayed a passion to

---

121 John Whitmore. *Coaching for Performance* (Nicholas Brealey, 1992), p. 97.

constantly address their weaknesses. It makes perfect sense to build on strengths, mould the role to fit capability, and delegate to others what we don't do well.

None of this means that a philosophy of building on success makes a performance limitation, misalignment with the organization's values, or an Achilles heel any less of a problem. That your car has three inflated tires doesn't mean you can ignore the one with a nail sticking out. The fact that the head of international markets is a one-of-a-kind strategist in no way excuses rude, intolerant, or abusive behaviour. The dilemma: **Any** leadership behaviour that inhibits the success of others is an Achilles heel!

Part two: The conversation

So far, so good, but what if the context doesn't provide a helpful backdrop? What if the type of leadership enacted overall in the organization is dominated by a need to micromanage? What if I have just taken over a dysfunctional team? What if my boss talks a good game, but when the tough decision has to be made, doesn't always provide a great deal of support? The answer: Work with what you've got. When the organization overall lacks a strong performance ethos, that **you** have the tough conversation becomes even more important.

In the midst of confusion, leadership is (1) bringing a laser-like focus to the outcomes demanded, (2) celebrating and building on success, and (3) being totally consistent in outlining and managing the **consequences** of failure.

In my experience, there are four distinct stages to successfully landing the tough conversation:

1. Lay out the issue.

2. Listen to what the employee has to say.

3. Pass ownership to the employee.

4. Move to the end game.

1. Lay out the issue.

> Respond quickly. Be consistent. Express the performance concern in unambiguous terms. As you lay out the issue, don't apologize, appear tentative, say you're sorry about the situation, or suggest you are there "to help." Helping doesn't help. It merely delays the inevitable. By inference, don't make the issue under discussion **your** problem (as in, "Let's figure out how **we** address this"). That doesn't mean

you lack empathy and caring. You care. You care enough to be candid. You care enough to make sure there is **no** confusion about who owns the problem. You care enough to lay out the consequences of failure.

> The delivery of the message is as important as the content. Be conscious of your tone of voice. Never appear to be angry or hurried. Look the employee in the eye. Believe that the change demanded **will** happen.

> Reinforce **why** the issue is important, e.g., values, commitment, impact on the team, sales lost. Revisit the agreed goals. Emphasize the nature and meaning of "commitment."

That your car has three inflated tires doesn't mean you can ignore the one with a nail sticking out.

> Provide "evidence" to support your point of view. Follow the **3-I**s rule: (1) **I**ntended outcome/goal – what was agreed; (2) **I**ncident – the context, what unfolded, observed behaviour; (3) **I**mpact – the final outcome and how others were affected. Emphasizing the agreed goals links behaviour to performance. The conversation is not about the individual; it's about performance. Be specific. To the extent possible, support your perception of the critical incident with data, information, and facts. Be current – unless it was discussed at the time, going back several months makes you part of the problem.

> Although it is suggested in much of the literature, avoid "Here is how I feel about the issue." Talking about how you **feel** makes it personal. It's not about you – it's about performance. Moreover, the "feelings" conversation can start to push the conversation down a slippery slope – away from performance and towards personality and character.

> Use "I" language wherever possible. "This is what I have witnessed." "This is how your behaviour comes across to **me**." The use of "we" introduces a degree of uncertainty into the conversation. The employee's internal conversation starts to sound like, "I know not **all** the others feel that way." The more specific your facts, the easier it is to focus on the needed change of behaviour going forward. Avoid presenting your point of view as though you were omnipotent. Be tough-minded, make your point, but create enough space for the employee to have their say. "What I have witnessed"

is far more palatable than "Here is what you did." And don't forget, what we seek to change (or are qualified to address!) is the employee's observable behaviour, not character. You're a manager, not a therapist.

2. Listen to what the employee has to say.

> Listen! Be fully present! Don't interrupt, other than to seek clarification. Don't signal your agreement or disagreement with the points being made through your overt body language, such as shaking your head. Don't respond to what is being suggested until you have heard the employee out. In pointing out where you disagree, avoid argument by supporting your point of view with "evidence." If the information you have drawn together appears to be inaccurate, adjourn and revisit the issue later. If you do your homework, this will not be necessary.

> Don't get drawn into an "it's not my fault" conversation. These represent a communication black hole from which there is no escape. Classic amongst these being: "The real problem is ..." "We could do that if only ..." "No one told me about ...". Don't get trapped into a conversation that blames someone not in the room.

> Challenge vague or ambiguous language. Ask questions along the lines of: "Explain what you mean." "Be more specific." Don't let the employee confuse the issue by introducing opinions presented as facts. A tactic much loved by politicians, if the "opinion" isn't challenged, it sits in the middle of the table as if it were a fact: "We will never be able to get new products to market faster than we do now" is an opinion! When somebody says, "The real facts of the matter are ... ," in all probability you are about to hear an opinion.

> Remember, if the issue under discussion is behaviour that even hints at lack of integrity, don't just be tough-minded. Be rough-minded.

3. Pass ownership to the employee.

> This is the most important part of the conversation. The challenge: to pass accountability to the employee. Having defined the issue and listened to the employee's response, ask, **"What are you going to do about it?"**

> In listening to the employee's suggested "solution," gauge if their view of the issue represents a **"doesn't know how to do"** or **"won't do"** dilemma. A **"won't do"**

predicament calls for a clear message: a reiteration of the behaviour demanded **and** clarity around the resulting consequences if the change being presented isn't enacted. Concerns around not living the organization's values, more often than not, represent a "won't do" issue. Even if the individual consistently delivers results, if he/she fails to live the organization's values,[122] you are faced with a "power struggle" **you** cannot afford to lose. Confront **"won't do"** issues head on! Coaching, mentoring, and, for that matter, support from the rest of the team all build on a presumption that the employee wants to change. Where that **will to change** is missing, managing consequences becomes not just your best, but your only meaningful option.

› If you believe that the employee has the capability (and motivation) needed to address the issue, determine if all of the skills demanded are fully present. If the employee has the skills and knowledge needed, start from the assumption that they know what needs to be done and how to do it. Most of the time they do!

› Ask questions that draw out next steps. Don't make suggestions. Don't "tell" the employee what to do. Avoid questions that telegraph the "answer" you are looking for. Use silence to provoke new thinking. If the employee has exhausted all of their own resources, then and only then move to problem solving. Jointly explore possible options. Share your own experience. Push the employee to build on the ideas being presented. Check for buy-in. Only as a last resort "tell" the employee what you want him/her to do. If "telling" becomes necessary, re-emphasize **why** the change is necessary and lay out **specifically** what they need to do.

4. Move to the end game.

› Establish goals going forward. Define specifically what needs to happen and by when. Agree on "the how." Write it down. Emphasize (again) the nature and meaning of a "commitment."

› Show belief in the employee's ability to "make it happen." Offer support. Emphasize the value to the employee in making the change (e.g., financial rewards, growth, personal opportunity).

› Establish milestones. Review progress against those milestones. Follow through. Encourage, affirm, and go out of your way to recognize and celebrate early success.

---

122 For "values" also read "leadership competencies."

> If the agreed outcomes are **not** delivered, work on the presumption that the employee is either in the wrong role or in the wrong organization. Not to act is to fan the flames of entitlement. Not to act is to demotivate your top performers. Not to act is to delegate the standards against which performance is judged to the employee. Not to act is to make a statement that as a leader **you** are either in the wrong role or in the wrong organization.

We live in challenging times. We need **everyone** to deliver. We need **every** leader to make managing performance an overriding **daily** priority. And that means carrying out those so-easy-to-put-off tough conversations. Not to act is to act. Not to act is a form of permission. Not to act is to embrace marginal performance as a way of life.

At the worst of times, people look to a leader. The more uncertain things are, the more unstable the marketplace, the more an ability to manage performance becomes central to how leaders are judged. Leadership is about steering towards a better tomorrow. It's about marshalling people behind a common cause. It's about nurturing growth and learning. And it's about confronting those who, by their actions, signal they are on a different path. When performance is found wanting, when the actions of any single person on the team start to strip hope out of possibility, leaders **must** lead!

If the ongoing performance management process were complemented by genuine insight into how to have the tough conversation, we would:

_____

_____

_____

_____

_____

_____

As an organization, to make the tough conversation part of the fabric of the business, we need to:

_____

_____

_____

_____

_____

_____

Starting now, beyond what I already do, to ensure that I deliver the tough conversation as effectively as possible, I am committed to:

_____

_____

_____

_____

_____

Part three:
ENGAGING THE HEART
AND
ENRICHING
THE SPIRIT

"Most of us have jobs that are too small for our spirit."
– *Studs Terkel*

Chapter eight:
TO SUCCEED IS TO KNOW
WHY BEING THE BOSS ISN'T

In an upside-down world

Yesterday, leaders sought "to be in charge." Today, leaders have to know how to get out of the way.

The narrative of the trapped mind

"This is very much a warrior culture – apologize too often, admit to mistakes, and you're seen as something of a wimp."

"Hiding your light under a bushel isn't my style. My experience is that if you don't promote yourself, you don't get promoted."

"My BlackBerry is my lifeline. If I'm not in the loop, I'm not in the game. If it's perceived that I'm not in the game, I know people will start to ask if I'm needed."

"Being self-effacing and generally subordinating myself to the aggressive 'winners' around here is a poor career strategy."

"Look, things are so chaotic in my area that coming across as being anything other than a tough and demanding boss simply wouldn't get me anywhere."

The rest of the story …

Humility is the unbreakable thread that runs through any and all acts of inspirational leadership.

To succeed is to know why being the boss isn't

"Leaders wedded to 'being right,' who feel the need to impose their will, who enjoy 'being in charge,' rarely hire those whose natural style is to challenge 'the boss.'"

We live in a world where a day without a surprise – is a surprise. Leadership, as a result, means creating a business culture that is "change-ready." The capacity to anticipate what lies over the horizon, to see emerging patterns before others, to take risks, to know how to fail fast, to work successfully with people who are different from ourselves – all loom large in the leadership qualities demanded. In my own ongoing conversations with successful leaders, however, in addition to those mentioned, one essential leadership characteristic stands out: **humility.**

Humility is generally taken to mean (1) a modest opinion of oneself generally and, more specifically, (2) the avoidance of an over-inflated opinion of one's rank and/or status. C. S. Lewis said, "Humility is not thinking less of yourself but thinking of yourself less."

What is clear is that the higher the pedestal a leader seeks to stand on, the less opportunity there is, literally, to look people in the eye; the more difficult, therefore, it becomes to build trust. Arrogance, a sense of self-importance, power derived from the formal definition of the role may stroke the ego, but in the world we find ourselves in they clearly don't have very much to do with leadership.

By comparison, those who display HUMILITY:

> **H**ire people who are better or different from themselves. Leaders wedded to "being right," who feel the need to impose their will, who enjoy "being in charge," rarely hire those whose natural style is to challenge "the boss." Leaders who embrace humility go out of their way to hire people smarter than themselves. Moreover, in that they also feel comfortable in admitting their own limitations, they work hard to bring new team members on board who bridge or fill the hiring manager's own shortcomings.

> Humility is to work from the belief that the hiring process is a craft that has to be constantly evaluated and honed. It is to avoid being trapped by the misplaced assumption that "fit" can be judged from a two-hour interview. It is to do the

hard recruitment work. Humility is to be wedded to diversity. It is to know that having people on the team who come from a different background or culture adds immeasurably to the potential success of the team. Assessing evolving trends, understanding customer expectations, the level of agility overall, idea generation, and the quality of decision making all trend upwards when diversity is factored into what it means to be part of a successful team.

The humility index: When and in what way did you recently share with your team what you perceive to be your own blind spots? Do you have a successor? During the past year, in what ways have you upgraded your hiring and interview skills? Describe specifically in what ways you have made diversity central to how you define hiring success?

Understand that leadership isn't a right or a function of title. Those who display humility recognize that guiding the team is a privilege that has to be earned **every day.** It is an opportunity to serve that rests on the goodwill, respect, and trust of those being asked to follow. Is that important? It is in an age when no one (emphasize, no one) can succeed without a supportive team. It is when access to technology and specialist know-how means that the team leader is but first amongst equals. It is when the next generation of employees are unlikely to make a commitment to the firm unless they see a compelling reason to stay.

> *Those who display humility recognize that guiding the team is a privilege that has to be earned every day.*

Those who see leadership as a privilege are comfortable "not knowing." They understand that being unsure offers the possibility to find a new way, whereas being certain but on the wrong path is a seductive form of self-delusion. Humble leaders work from the assumption that the best way forward lies not with themselves but with those in the room. They go out of their way to ask naive questions. They find creative ways to "test" talent. They understand that there is a symbiotic relationship between risk and growth and that, without personal reflection, there is no learning.

The humility index: Are you a "CrackBerry" sufferer? Do you feel naked when you're not in touch? Do you feel insecure when you don't know exactly what is going on? Are you stifling the freedom to act? Are you making decisions that are rightfully the prerogative of those who report to you? When you work with people from a different generation, in what ways do you modify your behaviour to ensure that you connect as effectively as possible? How often do you take time out for reflection?

> **To be humble means that leadership is never rooted in the leader's personal success or reputation.**

Manage up and lead down. To be humble means that leadership is never rooted in the leader's personal success or reputation. Humility is to speak with one's own voice. It means to shed the mask that hides the real self. Leaders who display humility instinctively know that the right path is rarely the easy path. They stand up for their people. Always! They push back when the goals for the team are unclear. When "speaking to power," when the tough question needs to be asked, they have the courage to step forward. Communicating up: They deliver the tough message. Communicating down: They focus on the outcome, the challenge, the "joy" of winning, and what's possible – not on what's holding us back. To be humble is to make fairness in all things a way of life. It is to always put people first when questions of fairness arise. It is to work from the belief that anything that strips people of dignity is, in its own way, an act of violence.

The humility index: How do you know you deal with people consistently? Describe your leadership point of view. Think of those times when the "real you" turns up. Conversely, are there times when you project only what you perceive those in the room want you to be? What is different about those situations?

Inspire others to give of their best. Humility is the unbreakable thread that runs through any and all acts of inspirational leadership. It's tough to inspire anyone if the outcome being described is all about the needs of the person standing at the front of the room. No matter how seductively presented, little derails early signs of enthusiasm more effectively than a leader who strives to make "This will make me look good" come across as a "This will be good for you" communication. Even the "techie" at the back of the room, covertly listening to gangsta rap on his iPod, will have figured it out before the second track of his Snoop Dogg classic has kicked in.

Inspiration is a spark ignited by challenge that has meaning, by the nature of the contribution – by giving, not taking. Others follow when they share a sense of worth in the purpose, when they are at one with the course being charted, and when the ongoing dialogue clearly shows that the leader cares. Team members are inspired when the organization they work for is admired in the community, when the work they do lives after they have gone. That being said, although inspiration is enshrined in "the dream," it is only in part aspirational. Those who inspire deliver a practical and empowering message that finds full flower in the focus and energy of those charged with day-to-day delivery. It's an emotion-laden framing of tomorrow's possibility that fills the white space on the organization chart with an unwavering sense of urgency. Today!

The humility index: What are you personally inspired by? If asked, what would those around you suggest inspires you? In what ways do you amplify how the work your team is engaged in makes a difference in the lives of others?

Listen. To listen is to first create the context for people to speak from truth. From the leader's perspective, this means a willingness to extend trust. It means putting the needs of others first. It means abandoning even the subtlest suggestion of appearing, or wanting, to be the smartest person in the room. It means a willingness to say, "I don't know" or "I was wrong." It means, when needed, delivering a heartfelt apology. It means acting on the belief that **every** conversation is a listening opportunity. To be humble is to listen to one's own voice. It is to display generosity of spirit not just to others, but to one's self. To be humble is to know how to forgive ourselves.

The humility index: When did you last apologize? When did you last say, "I don't know?" In what situations do you fall into the trap of wanting to appear to be the smartest person in the room?

Instill a sense of pride in the things that are working. To be humble is to pass the torch. It's to identify and ignite the flame of possibility in those who will come next. It's to cameo the success of those who do the work. It's to project an unwavering sense of personal integrity. It's to surface and connect everyone on the team with their own story. It's to emphasize with those you coach and mentor that if they are not living their own story – they are living someone else's.

> *Humility is to help others shed the blindfold of inadequacy and let them see beyond what they assumed was possible.*

Humility is to help others shed the blindfold of inadequacy and let them see beyond what they assumed was possible. It's to recognize that the single most powerful tool any leader has is the simple act of affirmation. Conversely, humility is the perfect weapon to combat complacency. To lead is to face the day ready to do battle with those who already have the answer, with those who find a new question to be an inconvenience. Humility is to realize that "being the best" or "being first" is a fleeting measure realized by looking back at what has already happened.

Humility opens the door to curiosity. Curiosity, in turn, is energized by the belief that there is always a better way. Leaders who display humility are never troubled by the "not invented here" syndrome; they are quick to improve on what the competition does and do so at a level of excellence. Humility is to realize that tomorrow's harvest depends on how well the ground is ploughed today. It is to know that, like a good wine, a new idea tastes better when it is allowed to "breathe" before being served. It is to work from the assumption that early failure is often the price to be paid for long-term success.

The humility index: Name three people you admire in your own organization. What have you learned from each of them? What can you still learn? What organization do you admire? What have you done recently to learn from their experience?

Take the time to invest in others. Humility isn't just a state of mind; it's a state of being. It's learning from hard-won experience. It's to recognize and then nurture the best in others. It's to knowingly push those with talent to the very edge of their comfort zone – then stop them from falling if they take a step too far. It's to take pride in what the team has achieved. It's to share how and when you stumbled in your own career and what you learned from it. It's to be a mentor. It's to seek "reverse mentoring" opportunities.

Humility is to provide opportunity, step back, be patient, and then deliver feedback devoid of ego. Unhealthy ego is displayed by leaders who have a propensity to use sentences that start with the word "I." Unhealthy ego begets manipulation in its many subtle forms. Manipulation is the self-serving realm of the insecure. Humility is to be fully cognizant of the reality that someone new to the team sees with a fresh set of eyes. Humility is to invest time in the person on the team who is the most different from you – not with a view to change them, but with an underlying respect that leads to genuine sharing.

Humility is to be the easiest person on the team to confront and the most difficult to steer in a new direction when the team's integrity is on the line. It's to let the customer have the last word and the most junior member of the team have the first. It is to have the least to say at the meeting and then work the hardest to deliver what was agreed. It's to praise others as part of any and every presentation. Humility is to know that, regardless of personal performance, success is to help others on the team to "up" their game. It is to use self-deprecating humour to reduce tension. It is to ask questions that reinforce both the way forward and the personal qualities of those charged with getting there. A leader with humility is easy to identify: the first one to send a congratulatory letter and the last one to celebrate when a talented rival stumbles.

The humility index: Think about your most recent presentation. In what ways did you go out of your way to recognize and praise the contribution of others? Who is mentoring you? Who do you mentor? What do you take away from those experiences?

> **Being humble means sailing away from yesterday's safe harbour.**

Yearn not for that which was. Being humble means sailing away from yesterday's safe harbour. It is to know that beginnings start with endings and that yesterday's solutions rarely address tomorrow's problems. It's to be comfortable with who and where you are. It's to be in the moment. It's to savour the moment. It's to live life, not with a regret for what might have been, but with a sense of anticipation for what's to come. It's to take pride in the fact that as you get older, you're getting better. It's to work from the belief that the best work you will ever do lies in the future. It means recognizing that every question is a new question.[123] It means knowing how to straddle and work successfully in different cultures. It is to know that in the centre of any and all complexity lies an elegant pattern.

To be humble is to be wedded to simplicity both in communication and ways of working. Humility is to recognize that right-brain, intuitive, experienced-based wisdom is a gift from the gods; and that knowing when and how to step back and let others take the lead is the true mark of leadership mastery.

---

123 This is a modern variation of Heraclitus' famous statement, around 500 BC, that "you can't step into the same river twice."

The humility index: Describe specifically what you have successfully let go of in the past three months. Outline what are you currently working to let go of.

Being self-effacing doesn't imply lacking confidence. Standing back to allow others to stand on the winner's podium doesn't infer that the passion to win is somehow compromised. The absence of arrogance doesn't equate to lack of pride. Being humble shouldn't be confused with being hesitant, withdrawn, or slow to act. Nor does it imply lack of mental toughness or assertiveness.

Be it an idea, a product, a service, or our own merits, to succeed in life we all have to learn how to sell. Traditional sales training focuses on features and benefits: "Buy from us because we are better than the others." More enlightened, for that matter more successful, sales initiatives eschew the words "I" and "we" and, in doing so, emphasize that it's "all about the customer." That is to say, what the customer wants to buy is way more important than anything we want to sell. To be masterful in front of the customer is thus about humility: It's not about me, it's about the capacity to serve.

A while ago I visited a well-known fishing lake. The guide who attended to us wore an impressive vest depicting numerous fishing prizes and competition wins. Unfortunately, he didn't know how to stop competing, and at every "hole" he threw his bait in first. It goes without saying that not only did he have the biggest catch, but he also had the best time. We haven't been back!

Ask yourself, who would **you** follow? A humble and truly inspiring guide, or someone who goes out of the way to let you know how successful they are, who throws their bait in first, whose default conversation opener is "I" and whose personal need to catch the most fish sucks the energy out of the boat.

Remember, humility isn't a state of mind ... it's a state of being. Be humble!

Humility means ...

The needs of the tribe ("Us") – not the quest for tribute ("I")

Doing the right things – not being right

The outcome – not the occupant

Self-awareness – not self-interest

Being in the moment – not merely being in the room

Attitude – not altitude

A great question – not a clever answer

To listen – not the need to be listened to

To inspire – not to conspire

To collaborate – not criticize

To be the change – not manage change

Power-to – not power-over

Diversity – not dependency

Meaning – not manipulation

Honesty – not hubris

Making a difference – not making a reputation

Empathy – not ego

Coaching – not coercion

Being tough-minded – not tough on people

If humility were an ever-present quality in how leaders around here act, we would:

_____

_____

_____

_____

_____

_____

As an organization, to make humility central to how leaders think and act, we must:

_____

_____

_____

_____

_____

_____

_____

Starting right now, to ensure that, even more than it is currently, humility is clearly part of how I deal with the world, I need to:

_____

_____

_____

_____

_____

_____

Chapter nine:
TO LEAD IS TO LISTEN

In an upside-down world

Yesterday, leaders needed to know the answer. Today, they need to know the right question to ask – and, no less important, how to listen to the answer.

The narrative of the trapped mind

"To be honest with you, I think I am already a pretty good listener."

"There are some people, no matter what the situation, who turn me off. My response: I tune out."

"I know I should become a better listener and some of the time I do work on it, but when I'm in 'emergency mode,' listening seems to go out the window."

"In front of the customer, it's important to get across why you're better than the competition. I push the product and then I shoot down the customer's objections. And, guess what, I am pretty good at it!"

"Building rapport is interesting in some situations – but I don't like to give up control. I need to be myself!"

The rest of the story …

Listening is fundamental to discovering who we are: When we listen with intensity to someone else, we also listen to ourselves.

To lead is to listen

"We improve the quality of the listening experience immeasurably when our body language says to both the speaker and those present, 'What you are saying is important to me.'"

Niels Bohr, the eminent twentieth-century Danish physicist, was fond of saying, "How wonderful that we have met with a paradox. Now we have some hope of making progress."[124] Business life is full of paradoxes: Think long-term while, at the same time, respond to the aggressive, short-term demands of the capital markets; reduce costs but grow the business; nurture diversity, but build a common culture; be tough on those who don't live the values, but encourage risk taking; be focused, but strive to create agility; demand more by way of performance, but be conscious of the need for balance in people's lives.

The learning that Bohr spoke of comes from seeing a paradox, not as a binary choice between opposites, but as the opportunity to see the overall challenge from a new perspective. By replacing the "but" with an "and," one is forced into not just a creative solution, but a different mindset.

Nowhere is this more apparent than in the need for successful leaders to both move quickly **and** take the time to listen. Or, as Peter Drucker pointed out, fifty years ago leaders knew the answer; today they ask great questions. Asking a great question without stopping to listen to the answer is, of course, about as useful as throwing an anchor over the side without a rope or chain attached.

> *At no time in the past have leaders been faced with today's volume of background noise.*

The dilemma: At no time in the past have leaders been faced with today's volume of background noise;[125] with the level of access to people we do not meet; with the reality that a multicultural team is the norm. Although listening is more important than ever, at no time have there been more barriers. The good news: Opportunity beckons. The not-such-good news: When we look back five years from now – considering the growing trend of ever-more ways to grab the consumer's attention – today will seem like the good old days.

Every decade or so, those smart enough to design the protocols necessary to conduct listening "tests" with leaders, announce that our listening proficiency is, more or less, dysfunctional.

---

124 As quoted in Ruth Moore, *Niels Bohr: The Man, His Science, & the World They Changed* (Alfred A. Knopf, 1966), p. 196.

125 In 2007, to eliminate what Mayor Gilberto Kassab called "visual pollution," the city of São Paulo, Brazil, issued a ban on all outdoor advertising. The mayor argued that consumers were subjected to more than 3,000 "unwanted" advertisements each day.

Numbers that describe overall listening proficiency of 30%, or less, are commonplace. Put another way, in relation to its importance, our listening efficiency goes down every year.

There is a positive side. In much the same way that we know most of us are poor listeners, we also know what outstanding listeners do that makes them special. We know the difference that makes a difference. And lest we forget, if you want people to listen to you, first you have to show that you can, and do, listen to them.

Why don't we listen?

We don't listen when we make subconscious choices about who we perceive as being worth listening to. People who we deem to be less intelligent, less experienced, who have only tangential knowledge of the issue, or those who don't share our beliefs tend to be judged as being of marginal value. We often make a similar judgement about those whose use of language or dress signals that they hail from a different tribe.

> *To be a leader is to actively seek out those who disagree with us.*

We tend to avoid those who make our life difficult – those who make us angry, and those who ask the questions that make us uncomfortable. To be a leader is to actively seek out those who disagree with us. To be a leader is to work from the assumption that the individual with the least to say invariably has the most to add. To be a leader is to listen most closely to the person on the team who frustrates you the most. To be a leader is to know that followership is a choice and that leading a team is an act of service. To listen is to serve.

If you have eight people on a team and they all think the same way, seven of them are redundant. We invariably gain most by listening to those who are most unlike us. Personal breakthroughs happen when we afford others the opportunity to push against our way of thinking.

Someone who comes to the issue for the first time brings not just a fresh perspective but, as often as not, a new way to see what is possible. The customer that we can learn from isn't defined by those we currently serve. Important as it is, new insight isn't limited to listening to the customer we lose. It is the customer we have never landed; it is the one who rejected our offering out of hand who often offers the most compelling evidence of new opportunity. *The paradox: The people we reject as being those who offer little value are invariably those we can learn the most from.*

Any latent sense of superiority is compounded by an educational system that tends to present listening as a passive communication role.[126]   When, for example, did you last read a school report that made a comment on your child's skills in listening?[127] All relationships ultimately are about power. Unfortunately, the "power role" is mistakenly assumed to be the one in the spotlight, the actor who delivers the soliloquy, the leader presenting the information. Nothing could be further from the truth. The appearance of power is not the same as actually having power. A professional actor will be quick to point out that delivering the lines is the easy part and that the real "art" lies in how the other players listen. If you are in doubt … go watch a truly skilled salesperson do their thing.

How do we become better listeners?

We listen when we get rid of distractions, when we use our whole body as an antenna, when we make an emotional commitment to be there. We listen when we put a hold on likely interruptions and spend a few moments ahead of time clearing the clutter from our mind. We listen when our pre-listening self-talk moves to full volume with a message that emphasizes, "The next few minutes is an invaluable learning opportunity." We listen when we put the needs of others ahead of our own.

> *We listen when we get rid of distractions, when we use our whole body as an antenna, when we make an emotional commitment to be there.*

The average person talks at a rate of about 125–175 words per minute. Meanwhile, we can listen at a rate of up to 450 words per minute.[128] We fill that "vacuum" by daydreaming, attempting to both be in the conversation and elsewhere, by thinking about how **we** are going to respond when the other person has stopped speaking ("script writing"). Listening isn't a spectator sport. Listening is an intense, full-bodied, emotionally involved, empathetic experience. Simply put, listening is hard work.

We improve the quality of the listening experience immeasurably when our body language says to both the speaker and those present, "What you are saying is important to me." When we lean in slightly and maintain good eye contact, we signal that we are fully present. When we reinforce a key statement with positive body language such as a slight nod of the head, we are letting the speaker and everyone else present know that the message is landing. And when we allow the speaker to pause and we resist the temptation to jump in, what we are projecting is that **we are listening**.

---

126 About 85% of what we learn involves listening.

127 Less than 2% of college students have had any training in listening.

128 Carver, Johnson, & Friedman (1970), quoted in Andrew D. Wolvin & Carolyn Gwynn Coakley, *Perspectives on Listening* (Ablex, 1993), p.45.

The intensity described comes with a soft edge. When we appear relaxed, we make the speaker more comfortable. Our willingness to smile is a measure of our openness. When we use a "gentle voice," we are emphasizing that this is a shared experience. When **selectively** we paraphrase, restate and, as appropriate, summarize what the speaker has said, we are projecting that we care.[129] Even when it is clear that the speaker has concluded, when we wait two beats before giving our own response (or question), we give emphasis to the speaker's message. (Interviewers on television – please take note!)

To listen is to care. Not to listen, to half-listen, to assume that you are the important party to the communication are arrogant and overt acts of disrespect that carry an unambiguous, collective message: "Get on with it, my time is more valuable than yours." And does the other person (and everyone else present) pick up on that message? Every time!

Masterful listening is to listen without judgment. It is to be receptive, not just to new knowledge, but to be open to new ways of being. Listening without judgment thus means first stripping away the self-important presumption of "knowing the answer." It is a level of listening that demands a willingness to be truly open. It is a level of attentiveness that is only possible for those who have the capacity to be emotionally "still."

Listening mastery means constantly striving to reach the next level. It is ongoing learning that starts with a simple question, "What is the one thing that I can do which will make the greatest difference to my listening?" To grow as a listener is to write at the top of every page on the notepad you are using, "I will listen." To grow as a listener is to rate oneself at the end of every key meeting. Learning also means accepting feedback from others. It means finding the time to listen. It means asking others on the team how they would rate **your** listening skills. It means seeking input from the customer. More than anything else, of course, it means acting on the input.

What do great listeners do?

Great listeners are skilled in promoting listening when they themselves are speaking. They start with a smile, build rapport, establish eye contact, and adopt a relaxed posture. They put the key idea at the beginning of the sentence, weave in relevant stories and use the language of the listener. They use pace, tonality, and an ability to step outside of the communication dance and, in so doing, observe how the interaction is unfolding. All of this

---

129 A benchmark skill in most listening programs and invaluable where the parties to the conversations come from different cultures, in most situations, anything other than selective use of this simple technique tends to be somewhat annoying.

has an impact on how the audience's listening experience unfolds. Great listeners know how to work the room!

> *Great listeners are skilled in promoting listening when they themselves are speaking.*

The questions we ask can also go a long way to promote listening. Long, convoluted questions that contain several ideas work against listening. Questions that contain poorly chosen metaphors shut down listening (e.g., sports metaphors much beloved by many men turn most women off). Questions that begin with "Why" invariably trigger a defensive reaction that, in turn overpowers the intent and meaning that lie behind the question. Questions intended to open up dialogue but which contain the advice the speaker wants to introduce into the conversation signal, "I know best" and, in doing so, turn off the listener's attentiveness gene. Questions framed in the listener's language, that tap into those things the listener is proud of, that speak across rather than speak down to the listener – all serve to make the act of listening far more likely.

In a selling situation, a conversation that focuses on **you** is a surefire way to prompt the customer to look out of the window and think about the next meeting. Essential as it is to present a great product or unique service, success isn't merely about having a winning value proposition. The final "buy decision" is largely emotional; it is ultimately about how the customer **feels** about your offering and the people who stand behind it. The problem: orchestrating the right emotional "connection" is all but impossible if the customer's story remains untold. *If you don't listen, you can't sell!*

None of this implies that to listen we must lose, or disguise, who we really are. Listening isn't an act of manipulation. When someone else turns up, when any attempt to listen more effectively distorts our sense of self, we take away from, rather than add to, the listening experience. To become more effective as a listener is not about learning how to act in a way that contradicts our sense of identity. It is far more about reaching inside and amplifying qualities we already possess.

Listening is fundamental to discovering who we are: When we listen with intensity to someone else, we also listen to ourselves. The corollary, of course, is also true: Poor listeners invariably have an inflated sense of their own importance. When you spend most of the day listening to the "profundity" of your own speech, why would it be otherwise?

There are three levels of listening:

Interest: listening with a specific outcome in mind.

Intent: listening to understand the speaker's point of view.

Impact: listening to connect the conversation to the wider context.

Coaching, selling, mentoring, negotiating, interviewing talent, running a meeting, leading a team, working with customers, taking on a new role – all demand mastery at all three levels simultaneously. The conclusion: If you don't listen, you can't lead! And what sort of listener are you? See the Listening Tree questionnaire.

The Listening Tree

10
I ask for feedback on my listening.

9
I listen not for what is said, but for what is intended.

8
As a signal of respect, I go out of my way to use the speaker's words.

7
I pay attention to the speaker's non-verbal language and I do not interrupt.

6
I consciously do not allow myself to "script write" i.e., I do not think about what I intend to say while the other person is talking.

5
After listening to what someone has to say, I wait for two beats before I speak. In doing so, I signal that I am listening.

4
To listen is to be there! When I know that an opportunity to listen is coming up, I put a hold on interruptions and spend a few moments actively clearing the clutter from my mind.

3
As part of my listening agenda and, when possible, I go out of my way to build physical rapport with the person speaking. This includes maintaining good eye contact and adopting a complementary posture.

2
I listen not just with my ears but with my whole body. I make this apparent by giving affirmative, physical cues to the speaker: leaning in slightly, reinforcing key statements with a slight nod of the head, smiling in appropriate places, and maintaining listening intensity even when the speaker pauses.

1
Before any conversation, I remind myself that prejudice, past experiences with the individual, and assumptions that I already know what the person is going to say, severely limit listening effectiveness. I also remind myself that listening, far from being a passive role, is the power position in any conversation. Thus, if the speaker is unable to get his/her points across, I have failed.

Self-Assessment

Think about a recent conversation and review your listening at each level (1-10). For every level where your response is "that's absolutely me" you gain 10%. If in any doubt, or if the statement describes you "sometimes," you do not score at that level.

Score

30% (or less) doesn't listen
40% listens out of self-interest
50% listens for knowledge
60% listens for meaning
70% listens to uncover wisdom
80% + mastery

If listening were an ever-present quality in how leaders around here act, we would:

_____

_____

_____

_____

_____

_____

_____

As an organization, to make listening central to how leaders think and act, we must:

_____

_____

_____

_____

_____

_____

_____

Starting right now, to ensure that I become a better listener, I will:

_____

_____

_____

_____

_____

_____

_____

Chapter ten:
TO LEAD IS TO CARE!

In an upside-down world

Yesterday, leaders got to the top because their prime skill rested in analysis, selling, technology, or knowing how to work the numbers. Today's successful leaders know that ultimately it's people who count.

The narrative of the trapped mind

"I care, but I don't always show that I care."

"This isn't how I was trained. This isn't how I perceive successful leaders act."

"I would love to make things simpler. We work to simplify, but external events seem to always add levels of complexity that we find difficult to strip out."

"I act in the right way. I don't always say the right things at the right time."

"I ask members of my team for feedback. I'm not always sure that what people tell me is what they really believe."

The rest of the story …

To care is a deep-rooted, genuine, consistent way to be.

To lead is to care!

"If you wear the mantle of leadership, people need to **know** *that you care."*

What makes a leader? High on any agenda – using a phrase from Warren Bennis – is that, "Leaders are dreamers with a deadline." **John F. Kennedy's** dream leading to man's first steps on the moon is a classic example. The capacity to see what others cannot see while, at

> *To care is a deep-rooted, genuine, consistent way to be.*

the same time, remaining humble plays a central role – **Gandhi.** Energy and passion[130] are clearly essential – **Teddy Roosevelt.** Mental toughness and tenacity are important – **Margaret Thatcher.** Compassion and a generosity of spirit – **Nelson Mandela.** The deep-rooted and unshakable belief that no matter what the pundits, critics, and "experts" might suggest – *it will happen* – **Sergio Marchionne.**[131] And in a boundaryless world, the capacity to operate in different cultures cannot be ignored – **Jorma Ollila.**[132]

What makes a leader? To create and share the dream are clearly part of it, as are humility, energy, passion, mental toughness, tenacity, belief, and cultural agility. But what lies at the heart of it? What is it that takes people on a journey they would not otherwise attempt? The overwhelming evidence[133] is that when everything else is stripped away, when you get to the very essence of what it means to be a leader, to lead is to care! Think no further than **Bill and Melinda Gates.**

Leadership is, and has always been, about followership. As such, leadership is a sacred trust. A trust that has to be won every single day. People follow a leader who cares; someone who is more than a figurehead, more than an instrument of shareholder value, more than the manifestation of a set of competencies. Not someone who cares one day and not the next. Not someone who cares for some people and not others. And not someone who thinks that they care. If you wear the mantle of leadership, people need to **know** that you care.

To care is a deep-rooted, genuine, consistent way to be. Moreover, the greater the need to release the talent of those on the front line, the greater the need for caring leadership. To care is to work from the assumption that the world will (not might!) unfold in unpredictable

---

130 **Pass–inspiration–on.**

131 CEO of both Fiat and Chrysler.

132 Jorma Ollila, Chairman of the Board of Directors of Nokia Corporation; Chairman of the Board of Directors of Royal Dutch Shell Plc.

133 Evidence that comes from having personally asked over 10,000 leaders in 20 countries to describe the best leader they have ever worked for.

ways. It is to realize that there is no such thing as sustainable competitive advantage and that unbridled belief in "the plan" is to be wedded to yesterday's solution. It is to know that only those who can see what isn't there can deliver what others suggest cannot be done.

To care is to be fully aware that without investors there would be no organization. It is to honour that trust and make each and every decision transparent. To care is to work diligently to create value for shareholders. It is to hold in high esteem those whose own hard work and continued support enable the organization to exist.

A business leader who cares can always point to where and in what ways he or she is making a positive impact on the environment. Caring is to put the planet ahead of profit. It is to realize that we live in a fragile ecosystem where every act has long-term consequences. It is to fulfill the responsibility that goes with being a citizen of this earth. It is to know that we are a fragile species that, if we continue to destroy our precious heritage, will not survive the next 200 years. Simply put: To care is to leave behind a world that our grandchildren and their grandchildren will be proud of. At a micro-level, caring means making health and safety a true business priority.

To care is to leave behind a world that our grandchildren and their grandchildren will be proud of.

To foster hope

Caring leadership is to foster hope, to dream, and to compete for other people's dreams. Caring starts from the belief that people are resourceful, resilient, and ready. To care is thus to rid the workplace of work that strips people of dignity. To that end, leaders who care work to create whole jobs [134] not simply as a means to improve productivity, but because it nurtures the human condition. To care is to believe that people want to produce quality work and that, given the opportunity, front-line employees will always strive to improve the processes that dictate how the work they do gets done.

To care is to continuously raise the bar. It is to have an unrelenting drive for improved results. It is to be committed to goals that others merely aspire to. It is to know that growth, in its many forms, is the wellspring of sustained success. To care is to make delivery a drum beat that is echoed in every presentation, team meeting, and coaching conversation.

---

134 A "whole job" is one that balances the employee's capability with the opportunity on hand.

The organization isn't an abstract idea – it's a living organism. To care is to know that, armed with tenacity and a vision, any one of us can make a difference. It is to understand that even those in secondary roles, if truly committed to the cause, **can** inspire others to join them on a quest that has meaning. To care is stop expressing frustration about what you can't do and start to focus on what you can do. Because caring and insight go hand in hand, caring leaders are quick to recognize the difference between someone who challenges the status quo and a team member stuck in complaint mode. To care is to act on that insight.

> *To care is to recognize that the "sweet spot" in creating the customer experience is where the brand promise, innovation and culture converge.*

To care is to understand that an organization's culture and marketplace competiveness are but different sides of the same coin. It is to understand that the work on culture is ongoing and not a weekend workshop or a one-day event. It is to know that work on strategy that isn't complemented by an equal investment of time and effort on culture is, in its own way, an act of tyranny. To care is to recognize that the "sweet spot" in creating the customer experience is where the brand promise, innovation and culture converge.

Caring is about balance. It means working to build alignment between strategic thinking and strategic doing but recognizing, at the same time, misalignment and the tension that results is often the source of breakthrough ideas. Balance means responding to the expectations of a new generation while avoiding a culture of "entitlement." It means giving equal weight to short-term actions and long-term thinking. It means embracing the future that we are part of creating whilst honouring the past. It's realizing that we can't step into new shoes until we take off the ones we are wearing. It is the wisdom to know that what isn't said is always more important than what is. To care is to bring people onto the team who act and think differently than we do.

To care is to know that, although when spoken aloud the two words may sound similar, there is a deep-seated difference between "cult" and "culture." The former describes a single point of view. The latter is about a collective mindset. One seeks to stamp out any and all dissent. The other is made stronger by those who challenge the order of things. One is about **the** leader. The other is about leadership. In that they have to address the problems of the day, both involve (their own form of) discussion. A healthy culture **also** orchestrates dialogue. Discussion is about closure. The end product is agreement.

Dialogue is about exploration, discovery, and insight.[135] Dialogue's product is trust. It's about surfacing better ways for those on the team to work together. In the hands of a skilled facilitator, exploration moves to play. In that it is not unknown for leaders to occasionally blur the difference between a cult and a culture, to care is to encourage, stimulate, and support dialogue.

To talk the customer's language

To care is to know that selling isn't really about selling. It is to uncover in what ways the seller can make the customer's business better. It is to talk the customer's language and, in doing so, gain insights into the customer's world. It is to anticipate the customer's emerging needs. It is to understand the customer's customer. It is to listen ... really listen to what isn't said. It is to coach the customer such that they better understand how your product or service unlocks new possibility. It is to respond with not just a solution, but with the best possible solution. To care is to strive to always deliver a little more than that agreed upon.

Caring is to make integrity a way of life. To care is to recognize that the customer's needs dictate *the what;* values underscore *the how;* pragmatism orchestrates *the where;* opportunity dictates *the when;* ... but it is integrity that defines **the why.** Integrity is manifest in high ethical standards, an emphasis on personal responsibility, and a supportive work environment. Integrity is caring for the workers in an outsourced factory in Honduras no less than for those who work in the company's own plants. It is asking the questions that some would prefer to avoid. It is a compensation approach that rewards contribution, not the size of the office. It's treating everyone the same, regardless of role or level. Honesty, transparency, moral courage, independence of judgment, impartiality, and fairness are words that capture the spirit of integrity. Power without its alter ego, integrity, is exploitation. Leadership without integrity is to live a broken promise every single day.

To care is to constantly strive to deliver value. It is to focus on the output and not rejoice merely because the cost of the input has been reduced. To care is to evaluate "success," regardless of the function, process, or intervention, by measuring the impact of the work undertaken on business performance. In a similar vein, to care is to ask for feedback, not only from those who see the world the way we do, but from those who walk a different path.

---

135 Peter M. Senge and others, *The Fifth Discipline Fieldbook* (Crown Business, 1994). p 386.

To care is to have pride in the product and share that pride with others. To care is to know that product reliability is sacrosanct. It is to bring truthfulness to the sales process and to honour the spirit, not just the letter, of any and all promises made. It is to continuously explore ways to enhance the utility of the company's product or service. To care is to act with the knowledge that reputation is hard won but easily lost.

To have a passion to serve

To care is to push back conventional wisdom, to embrace new ideas, and to provide space and freedom in order that the imagination of those who serve the customer can take flight. To that end, to care is to support those who have the courage and daring to go where others have not walked. To care is to bring the customer's voice to every key decision. It is to stand behind the brand. It is to make the brand promise[136] live not just in the customer's eyes, but in the hearts and minds of everyone in the seller's organization. It is to act on the belief that serving is more important than service. Service is what happens when something goes wrong. Serving determines how the customer feels about that response. Unfortunately, in English, "to serve" carries with it historical connotations of "class" that aren't always positive. In Finland, they have a far better word: *hinku* – a passion to serve. To care is to embrace *hinku*.

> *... to care is to support those who have the courage and daring to go where others have not walked.*

To care is to act in tune with the rhythm of the marketplace. It is to realize that the only thing that is unchanging is the increasing speed of change, and that victory is the prerogative of those who embrace and relish change.

To care is to work to become ever more adaptable, flexible, and fleet-of-foot. It is to know when and in what ways to trust our intuition. It is to understand that in a world where change is an ever-present reality, in-depth or extensive analysis is all-too-often an emotional safety blanket for those uncomfortable with risk.

To care is to know that although mass customization is the way of the future, in a world where people have limited time to shop, too much choice pushes the customer towards a simpler offering. To care is to strip out the barriers between supplier and customer. It is to recognize that in some situations collaborating with the competition ("co-opetition") is

---

136 See **Chapter three** for the difference between the brand image and the brand promise.

the best way forward. To care is to know that to be a partner is to share not only "the how" but also "the why." It is to keep any and all partners fully informed and to provide real-time access to information that is critical to the customer's needs. To care is to build organizational capability that focuses on the knowledge of knowledge. It is to ensure that when seasoned performers move on or retire, hard won insights about the business are not lost.

To strip out boundaries that limit possibility

To care is to constantly seek ways to strip out unwarranted complexity. For those who care, simplicity is found in unambiguous goals; in policies and procedures that prescribe only that which is absolutely essential; and in feedback that focuses on issues that the receiver can influence. Simplicity is realized when the customer finds the product or service easy to access and straightforward to use. To care is to understand that simplicity is, in the first instance, a state of mind. It is also to know that there is a world of difference between "simplicity" and "simplistic." One is to strive for elegant solutions. The other is to create a simple product/service but in doing so forgo fitness for purpose.

To care is to be a role model. It is to keep top of mind that action is influence. It is to be always conscious of how even small acts will be interpreted. It is to challenge the established order and, in doing so, give others permission to explore new ways to act.

To care is to be committed to the belief that the efforts of people working together far outweigh the value of any individual. To care is thus to work collaboratively, to enrich social and business networks, and actively share experiences to better satisfy the customer. In that the creativity of the human mind can always find ways to circumvent the unnecessary and the unwanted, to care is to know that even well-meaning attempts to control others are always self-defeating. To care is to eschew the trappings of proclaimed self-importance. It is to know that "status" is a state of mind that insecure leaders seek in order that they can maintain the illusion of being in charge.

To care is to strip out boundaries that limit what is possible. It is to act in the belief that unnecessary organizational levels destroy value, that the informal organization is always more important than that implied by the formal structure, and that failure to cultivate the grapevine is to provide a forum for those who may not care. To care is to work from the assumption that the most effective way to organize reflects the way that people, given a choice, would organize themselves. It is to understand that merger, takeover, and acquisition are exclusively financial terms and that when two (or more) enterprises combine, a new entity **always** emerges.

> *... how people
> learn is more
> important than
> what they learn.*

To care is to have a teachable point of view. It is to work from the assumption that *how* people learn is more important than *what* they learn. To care is to discover new ways to learn. To care is to learn faster than the competition. To care is to find the time to be *available* and the state of mind to be *present*. It is to ask questions that allow others to see the world through a new lens. It is to change the patterns of play. It is to love the maverick. It is to develop a successor who will be more successful in the role than we are.

To purge the organization of favouritism, nepotism, and prejudice

To care is to ensure that fairness is built into every key decision. It is to purge the organization of favouritism, nepotism, and prejudice. It is to stamp out ageism, sexism, elitism, and every other "ism." It is to work from the belief that a disability of the body doesn't imply a disability of the mind. It is to understand that a wheelchair may limit flexibility of movement, but it doesn't limit flexibility of thought, and that the only ceiling that matters – glass or otherwise – is the one that keeps out the rain. To care is to rightfully invest in those with high potential. It is also to recognize that those who aren't on a fast track are, nevertheless, an invaluable asset. To care is to realize that downsizing, work-related stress, the pace of change, and concerns about the economy carry not only economic consequences, but impact physical wellbeing.[137]

To care is to communicate not what people need to know, but what they have a right to know. It is to find out how people feel. It is to share feelings. It is to find the time to listen. It is to see the world through the eyes of others. To care is to ask for help. It is to offer help. It is to be compassionate when others lose their way. It is to offer advice only when it's asked for.

To care is to act on the belief that leadership is about building community. Community, in turn, speaks to how people share ideas; how groups with a common interest build on each other's success; and how the collective spirit of competition propels people to the next plateau of performance. Caring is to emphasize that community is not about everyone being the same, but about the coming together of those who share a compelling purpose. It is to

---

137 One study reported in *People Management* (May 2010), found that one in five employees believed that their job made them physically ill.

recognize that diversity isn't just a legal requirement; it's simply the smart thing to do. To care is know that the organization cannot thrive in a vacuum and that the road to societal and customer rejection is littered with those who attempted to gain competitive advantage by riding roughshod over the public good.

Caring is manifest in the passion to hire and promote the best. It is to strive to identify world-class talent management consulting partners. It is found in the knowledge that every hire decision is central to the legacy that a leader leaves behind. It is to work from the knowledge that when talent management is described as "something we need to do better," what is implied is a breach of fiduciary responsibility. To care is to know that any and all shortfalls in the talent management system are multiplied many times over.

To live in truth

To care is to appreciate that because something is difficult to measure doesn't mean it should be judged purely by how the tide of uninformed, subjective opinion happens to be running at the time. Collaboration, culture, the sense of urgency, tenacity, trust, motivation, teamwork, leadership potential, and the human behaviour that drives innovation are all fundamental building blocks of organizational success that, although difficult to measure, with flair and creativity can be, and should be, regularly assessed. Alternatively, to care is to also know that just because something can be measured doesn't necessarily mean it should be. To care is to recognize that more measurement means less meaningful measurement. To lead is to regularly review and decide specifically what needs to be measured and, just as important, what measurement is no longer of value.

> *To care is to recognize that more measurement means less meaningful measurement.*

To care is to be approachable. It is to be human. To care is the courage to say no. To care is to live up to the expectations of others on the team. It is to be the first to accept accountability when things go wrong and the last to seek praise or personal reward when a successful outcome has been delivered.

To care is to respect the truth. It is to live in truth. It is to be open and honest even when political expediency means that silence is the option others would choose. It is to realize that timing is everything. To care is to act on the belief that confronting a problem is the first step in overcoming it.

To care is to realize that leadership demands stamina. It means taking wellness seriously; exercising and eating right; taking all of your vacation days; and providing the opportunity for others to do likewise. To care is having the courage to become your own hero or heroine. To care is to know that when we look back on a race well run, lifestyle, family, and health will be deemed far more important than financial rewards. To that end, to care means letting the ones we love know that we care – and do so often. When all is said and done, leadership-of-self is our single most important priority. To lead is to care about ourselves.

Crime statistics in the UK make interesting reading. Crime in Northern Ireland overall is at least 30% lower than the rest of the United Kingdom. Offences that tend to involve a juvenile are especially meaningful. In crimes using a knife, for example, whereas there were 233 rapes in England and Wales, there were only 3 in Northern Ireland. Robberies using a weapon with a blade – in England and Wales there were 16,701; in Northern Ireland only 236. Causing actual bodily harm: 18,940 in England and Wales; 509 for Northern Ireland.[138]

The reasons for the comparatively low crime rate in Northern Ireland involve lower drug use, a stronger sense of family than elsewhere in the UK and, perhaps most significant of all, sweeping changes in the way juveniles are dealt with by the courts. As an alternative to custodial punishment, young offenders are given the opportunity to make amends to their victims. This can include a written apology, performing unpaid community work and, most impactful of all, a face-to-face meeting with the victim where the offender gets to hear the traumatic impact of their crime on the victim's personal life.

Accepting that Northern Ireland has a population of only 6.2 million compared to England and Wales where the combined population is 55 million, the Youth Conferencing Service, which has been in effect since 2003, appears to be remarkably effective – a clear case, perhaps, of the power of caring on one hand, and the inadequacy of punishment on the other.

Martin Luther King Jr. said, "Our lives begin to end the day we become silent about things that matter." When we stop caring, we stop being a leader. When we stop caring about others, we stop caring about ourselves. To be a leader is to care. To be an outstanding leader is to care deeply.

---

138 All figures for 2008/09.

50 ways to say you care

The actions listed below are of necessity incomplete. They are not the product of a lengthy research project, nor are they intended to provoke hours of anxiety-ridden contemplation. The 50 simple suggestions given are simply a way for you to think about what it means to be a caring leader. Go through the list carefully and reflect on what specifically you can do differently on Monday:

1. Manners, civility, and everyday courtesy make a simple but profound statement about the sort of person you are. They also say a good deal about the sort of organization you are a part of.[139] Insist that everyone who meets the customer – especially those who look the customer in the eye (e.g., at check-out counters) – go out of their way to say "thank you."[140, 141]

2. Make the first call of the day to the one person you would rather not talk to.

3. Take the time to apologize.

4. Know that it is far more important to be "interested" than to be "interesting."

5. Learn the names of the children of those who work directly for you.

6. Say "we" when describing the future and what we have been successful at. Use "I" when mentoring, delivering the tough conversation, and discussing an issue that you played a role in that didn't work out.

7. Take the time to find out what the others on your team see as important in their lives. Discover the real person.

8. Share your dreams – in doing so, you give others the permission to dream.

9. Give back. Work at the local soup kitchen. Help someone learn to read.

10. Care about yourself. Revisit your life goals regularly. Live a healthy lifestyle.

11. Ensure that presentations reflect the multigenerational mix of the audience. Use metaphors that resonate with their backgrounds and interests.

---

139 The fall-off in civility in society is in direct conflict with what we know about why people buy in general, and in retail selling in particular. When there is little difference between brands, when quality is given and where an abundance of variety ultimately confuses the buyer, what brings the customer back is the memory created by the buying experience. Harrods, the legendary British retailer, constantly reinforces the same sales message to all its staff: "Teeth lead to smiles and smiles lead to sales."

140 The earliest towns came into being in Mesopotamia between 9000 and 6000 BC. Those towns had no codified laws, no police, and courtesy was thus an important element of the human condition if people were to live in harmony. As a result, we are hard-wired to expect courtesy. "There you go," in my experience, the most common closing comment by someone serving the public, doesn't somehow have the same emotional impact as a simple "thank you" – a term that has resonated down the ages.

141 To understand the relationship between leadership and courtesy, view the movie Invictus. Set against the Rugby World Cup in 1995, Morgan Freeman's depiction of Nelson Mandela throws out a challenge to all of us who hold down a leadership role.

12. Attend and start meetings on time. Close them on time. Always!

13. When you ask someone to call you back, leave a time when you will be available.

14. Don't let those who report to you hear news – good or bad but especially bad – from others first.

15. Don't use e-mail if you can walk to the individual's office and talk to them personally.

16. Keep a diary. Find personal time for reflection. Encourage the team to spend time in reflection.

17. Embrace diversity. If the ethnic background of those on your team is less diverse than that of the people you serve, know there is work to be done.

18. Mark in your calendar religious holidays for other faiths. Go out of your way to share an appropriate salutation with those who interface with you who share that faith.

19. Take the time to learn about the history, geography, and traditions of the country of those who work for you or with you, and who hail from a part of the world that differs from your own background.

20. If you are making an overseas call, learn what time it is in that country *before* making the call.

21. Don't assume that people who are 55-plus are any less enthusiastic about the future, are less willing to invest in personal growth than a 35-year-old – or are any slower to learn.

22. Coach the people who work for you in how to coach. Provide opportunities for people on the team to coach each other, for example, as part of regular meetings.

23. Make health and safety a priority. Fund wellness classes. Ensure electrical leads are taped down. Hold regular fire drills. It's not just a matter of avoiding personal risk; the impact lies in making people aware that their health and safety is something you care about.

24. Care about the planet. Find ways that the environment plays a role in the decisions your team makes. Champion sustainability and social accountability.

25. Be vulnerable. Share your 360° feedback with the team. Admit mistakes. Share with your team the times you stumbled and what you learned from the experience. Ask for help. Admit when you are wrong.

26. Communicate from truth. Confront those on the team who, when the tough conversation or new ways to act are needed, deliberately muddy the water or default into their own agenda.

27. Become an extraordinary listener. Listen in the way you want to be listened to.

28. Ask the others on your team for feedback. Act on that feedback. Learn to let go.

29. Know that leaders are readers. Read. Encourage others on the team to read. As a team, choose a great book; review and reflect on the insights gained – one chapter at a time.

30. Help new members of the team find their way. Three issues, in particular, are important to someone joining the team: (1) the leadership point of view of the team leader one-level-up; (2) the culture the organization is seeking to create; and (3) why others, new to the organization, have stumbled.

31. Stay in touch with people's aspirations. Organize small group sessions within your area of responsibility. Have little or no agenda. The purpose: to uncover how they feel about (1) the organization, (2) the work they do, and (3) their personal growth and development aspirations.

32. Keep people up-to-date by writing an informative blog. Make sure the blog focuses on what people want to know – not on what you want to tell them. Remember, it's not about you!

33. Learn what it's like on the front line. Regularly spend time in the trenches: work in the call centre, serve in the retail outlet, go on sales calls, wait tables. Be humble. Go to learn. Write down what people tell you. Be seen to be writing it down.

34. Involve everyone on the team when hiring a new team member.

35. Go out of your way to find out why your best people stay. Make that underlying reason happen more often.

36. Stress work–life balance. Be a good example to the team. In doing so, you give each of them permission to orchestrate their own approach.

37. Stay in touch with employees who have retired.

38. Insist that when someone comes to you looking for an answer to a question that hasn't come up before that they have also thought through at least one potential solution. Assume that the coachee is complete, capable, and committed to the solution being offered.

39. Delegate. Stop making decisions that aren't yours to make. Allow the people who work for you to do **all** of their job. If you are the leader you need to be, your subordinates will make the same decision you would have done (or a better one).

40. Go to bat for the people who work for you. At the same time, if you are the team leader ask yourself, "In what ways have I contributed to the issue?"

41. Become a great storyteller. Share positive stories. Encourage others on the team to share positive stories.

42. Work to reduce the time people spend travelling; use video conferencing and other connectivity tools wherever possible.

43. Build 10% into everyone's role such that they can pursue (without boundaries or constraints) new ideas or better ways of doing things.

44. Understand what people on the team are struggling with. Attend workshops or courses on the issues facing the team. Run your own workshop.

45. Adopt a cause where the team can make a difference, e.g., organize a class at a local high school, support a seniors' home, build a kids' playground, attend a tree planting day as a group.

46. Respect people's downtime. Call a team member at home only as a last resort.

47. Go the extra mile when a team member (or one of their family) is dealing with a serious health issue.

48. Constantly look for ways to ensure the work people do (1) is unambiguously defined by way of goals and responsibilities, (2) is aligned with the individual's capability, and (3) evokes stretch and challenge.

49. Be true to yourself. Make sure the real you turns up – every day. Be consistent. Know that if people perceive you as being anything less than 100% authentic, they will not trust you.

50. Recognize that the basic currency of organization success is **the team.** Take time out as a team to reflect on how (1) team performance and (2) the relationships on the team can move to the next level. Remember that motivation is and can only be intrinsic and that asking is far more effective than telling.

If caring were an ever-present quality in how leaders around here act, we would:

_____

_____

_____

_____

_____

_____

As an organization, to make caring central to how leaders think and act, we must:

_____

_____

_____

_____

_____

_____

_____

Starting right now, to ensure that I come across as being even more caring than I do now, I will:

_____

_____

_____

_____

_____

_____

_____

Chapter eleven:
TO LEAD IS TO "CATCH PEOPLE DOING IT RIGHT"

In an upside-down world

Yesterday, leadership was all about waiting for things to go wrong and then acting (management **by** exception). Today, leaders understand the importance of amplifying and sharing what's working (management **of** exception).

The narrative of the trapped mind

"My team has come to accept that I will jump on them pretty hard if something goes wrong."

"My role is to get results, not run around telling people how great they are."

"The people who report to me don't need that!"

"I start the day off thinking I am going to be more affirming, but as the day unfolds and fixing becomes the focus, it's tough to draw out what's working."

"I know that people want to be appreciated, but my teams know exactly how I feel about each of them. I don't have to keep telling them how valuable their contribution is."

The rest of the story . . .

The meaning we draw from the world around us is itself a creative act.

To lead is to "catch people doing it right"

"Outstanding leaders are masters of positive feedback. How good are you?"

You can't separate innovation from risk taking – and people avoid risk if they lack confidence. Innovation is born of the confidence needed to paint outside the lines. The confidence to explore territory where others fear to go. The confidence to blur the difference between managing and being managed. The confidence that comes from knowing if things go wrong, the battle cry will be, "What can we learn from this?"

In any endeavour, self-confidence is an important and often critical ingredient of success. Without self-confidence, "play to lose" rules the day. Without self-confidence, the art of the possible falls prey to a myopic focus on the immediately attainable. Without self-confidence, boundaries defined by others describe where the action stops ... not where imagination begins. Without self-confidence, victory remains a "hoped for" possibility. Without self-confidence, coming second quickly becomes good enough.

> **Self-confident leaders are drawn to risk because they see risk as the gateway to growth.**

To be self-confident is to see the glass half full. Self-confidence is the inner belief that "I can and I will." Self-confidence is knowing that to play a small role in a successful project is more enriching than leading a noble failure.

Self-confidence – not self-delusion

Self-confident leaders are drawn to risk because they see risk as the gateway to growth. Self-confident people are, in particular, comfortable with emotional risk. They confront those whose actions serve their own purpose ... they push back if they believe the team leader is being less than totally honest ... they speak up in team meetings when what remains unspoken is holding the team back. By comparison, those who lack self-confidence wrap themselves in a cocoon of silence in the belief that blending into the background is a recipe for survival. The dilemma: Holding back, not speaking up, being satisfied with the way things are, is a mandate for mediocrity. Self-confidence breeds a "can-do" attitude. People who lack self-confidence go out of their way to broadcast even marginal success, and they cast around for someone to blame when things go wrong.

Self-confidence is not the same as self-esteem. The former is situational, while the latter is an enduring personality trait. Self-confidence is rightly the realm of successful leadership. Lack of self-esteem is best left to a health care professional.

Self-confidence shouldn't be confused with self-delusion. To be self-confident is to know one's self. It's to know one's limitations. Self-confident people ask for help simply because they don't spend their lives protecting their ego. For the same reason, self-confident people are equally quick to offer help – even if the individual in question is a rival. No less important, self-confident leaders do not long hold onto what might have been – where others see failure, they see untapped wisdom and future opportunity. To be self-confident is thus to fail fast and move on.

To be a leader is to be both personally self-confident and nurture self-confidence in others. The first is possible only if we strive to be who we say we are – willing to surface and then connect with our own inner self. Self-confidence in pursuit of someone else's dream is to build a house on a foundation of sand.

> *To be a leader is to be both personally self-confident and nurture self-confidence in others.*

Self-confidence is to measure one's performance against standards that define excellence. Building self-confidence in others is rooted in asking great questions and creating opportunities that allow others to better exploit their own underlying mastery.

Self-confidence is enacted in a climate where the leader seeks to catch people "doing it right." When the leadership approach amounts to little more than seeking to fix that which appears to be broken, self-confidence withers much as grass might if it were constantly weeded but not given water. Building on strength and capability expands the human spirit. Constantly emphasizing what is wrong is an ever-present reminder that failure beckons.

Self-confidence is anchored in our identity – it is part of who we are. That doesn't mean that self-confidence is a constant. Even the most optimistic of us flirts with the fear of failure. Even the most resilient of us is tempted to listen to self-talk that says, "Hold back! You may not be up to the challenge." To be self-confident is to be able to surface our self-doubts. To be self-confident is to have the courage to drag uncertainty from the depths of our unconscious self, confront that which holds us back, and negotiate a positive outcome.

Doubt and despair – or possibility and potential

How employees interpret what they hear is an important factor in how they act. Indeed, it can be argued that the meaning we draw from the world around us is itself a creative act. In the face of adversity, each of us can choose doubt and despair – or we can opt for possibility and potential. In confronting negative "self-talk," we are helped when success is reinforced through reflection and celebration. Outstanding leaders understand this. Outstanding leaders are masters of positive feedback, not because it makes people feel good, but because affirmation provides the weaponry we all need to stay positive in an uncertain and competitive world.

The evidence, however, is that people receive three to five times as many negative comments at work as positive. One study in the US found that over half the workers stated that they had received no recognition or praise in the past year. And consider the work of John Mordechai Gottman.[142] By studying the "microexpressions" that punctuate the conversation between a newly married couple, he can predict with 90% accuracy whether or not the couple will still be together in six years. His findings: If the ongoing interaction between the couple isn't skewed 5:1 in the positive, it can be taken for granted that a visit to a divorce lawyer lies in their not-too-distant future.

Leadership rooted in reality

One of the questions that invariably surfaces when affirmation is discussed tends to be along the following lines: "I understand the need to be positive, but we have a lot of tough issues to deal with here. Doesn't an attempt to make people feel good fly in the face of good old-fashioned honesty?" The answer: Leadership is rooted in reality. Affirmation is not about creating a Pollyanna-like atmosphere. To lead is to share the truth. Truth is not just what the leader knows, but – perhaps even more importantly – how they feel about what they know. Holding back, putting a spin on the facts, partial truth or conversations slanted to serve the leader's needs – all these destroy trust. No less damaging, an agenda that is a constant and repetitive litany of the things that need to be fixed destroys respect.

A not-uncommon comment from executives about affirmation is this: "I see the value of positive reinforcement as a tactic for middle managers, but at the top of the house we really don't have the time for this stuff." The counter-argument? Napoleon, for whom victory

---

142 Dr. Gottman is a professor emeritus of psychology at the University of Washington.

was everything, was the master of affirmation. He was quick to promote the brave. The more courageous the officer, the faster he could expect to be promoted. To battalions that had fought bravely, he awarded special flags. To the hundred bravest men in his army, he awarded damascened swords inscribed: "Given on behalf of the Executive Directory of the French Republic, by General Bonaparte to citizen...."[143] Like all of those who accomplish great things, Napoleon understood that passion lies not in the head, but in the heart. He knew that winning was far more about emotion than it was about the right plan.

It is also worth stepping back for a moment to consider an average day in the life of a typical employee. Assuming that one of the first things the employee does in the morning is read the newspaper, it can be taken for granted that the news will be dominated by problems and tragic events. Switching on the television will yield more of the same. Listening to the radio on the drive to work: same again. By the time the employee arrives at work, just to retain any degree of emotional sanity, they will have had to push a veritable mountain of bad news into a space marked: "Not my problem." Now let's move the day forward an hour. The employee is invited to a meeting and told that the company's sales over the preceding quarter were a disaster. Guess what! The tried and true defence mechanism kicks in. The bad news is filtered, rationalized, and depersonalized until it becomes yet one more piece of data ready to be filed away. Unless the employee has an emotional stake in the game. Unless the employee's feelings of self-worth and the organization's success are connected. Unless possibility and challenge are brought to the fore as often and aggressively as are the problems that arise. Simply put, every act of affirmation is an emotional investment that increases the likelihood that concerns and problems will be recognized, taken to heart – and acted on.

Are there any rules for affirmation? Not many, but what guidelines there are ... are important:

> Affirmation must be accurate, meaningful, genuine in the way it is delivered and well deserved. Anything less, and the leader is stepping into murky waters.

> The more specific the affirmation, the greater the impact.

> Affirmation must describe the overt behaviour (that which is observable) and not drift into comments about the individual (presumed beliefs, assumptions about attitude, conjecture around why the individual acted in a certain way). The rule: performance and not personality.

143 Vincent Cronin, *Napoleon* (HarperCollins, 1995), p. 154.

> Affirmation, by definition, should focus on the positive. With that in mind, affirmation should reinforce and point to the behaviour you want – not congratulate someone on the cessation of behaviour you don't want. When a habitually poor time-keeper has turned the corner, for example, the feedback should reinforce the merits of being on time and not extol the virtues of not being late. When someone has overcome the tendency to overspeak while someone else is speaking, the feedback should emphasize the quality of the individual's new communication skills and not dwell on giving praise for giving up a dysfunctional habit.

> Make the feedback fit the occasion. Gushing praise for a small, albeit successful act makes it tough to appropriately reinforce a major breakthrough.

> Timing is everything. The general rule: as close to the event being described as possible.

> Be sensitive – not everyone wants to be congratulated in front of the room. Sensitivity is especially important in a multicultural business environment.

> Change the patterns of feedback. Make affirmation a surprise. Find ways to reinforce the positive that the employee will not have anticipated. When people hear the same thing several times, it loses its potency.

> Factor in multigenerational differences. Gen Y employees and their younger cousins communicate through text messaging and social networking sites. Push affirmation into the space they recognize and respond to.

> Motivation is intrinsic. Use the employee's language. Find ways to reward positive behaviour that plays into the events, activities, hobbies, or causes the employee cares about.

During periods of uncertainty, organizations wisely question the assumptions that made them successful in the past. This leads naturally to the need to recast "the strategy" – always remembering, of course, that without the discipline of strategic implementation strategy, no matter how well formed, is but a pious hope. Learning and agility come into play because without new ways for employees to think and act, change is something the other guys do. In times of difficulty, what is often ignored is "spirit" – the meaning that lies behind the work. When we stumble, it's not the strategy that makes us rise. When things are tough, it's the spirit that enables us to climb yet one more mountain. Spirit! In good times, we take it for granted. In difficult times, we find we can't survive without it. Spirit lies in a shared dedication to the challenge; a sense of community with those whose support is needed; a dogged determination within the team not to fail; a one-for-all, all-for-all attitude; humour and playfulness;[144] celebrating early wins and, of course, self-confidence. Leaders who are masters of affirmation build organizational spirit. Those who are not come ill-equipped for tough times.

> *When we stumble, it's not the strategy that makes us rise.*

In June 2003, American golfer Jim Furyk won the 103rd US Open. Apart from the fact that his score of 272 for four rounds (or 72 holes) tied the lowest score by an Open winner, what was remarkable about Furyk was how untidy ("quirky" is how one newspaper described it) his swing was. And Furyk's response? "I was fortunate that my dad realized I wasn't very mechanical and let me play by feel. And we took the positive traits in my swing and tried to build on that. If I had taken my swing and tried to make it look textbook when I was a kid, I might not be sitting here today."[145] Scratch a winner, and you are likely to find not just learning born of experience, but the self-confidence that comes from timely affirmation.

Innovation, breakthrough thinking, and new ways to be aren't derived from simply hiring "good people." They are the outcome of allowing employees to make important decisions; creating a safe haven for controversial ideas to emerge; reinforcing the wider role the organization has in society; and viewing the business, not merely as a series of related value-adding processes, but as a living community. A community that nurtures the human spirit. A community that embraces and thrives in the positive.

Perhaps the best guidance for affirmation that I have read comes from a book mentioned earlier, *First, Break All the Rules* by Marcus Buckingham and Curt Coffman:[146]

> People don't change that much.
>
> Don't try to put in what was left out.
>
> Try to draw out what was left in.
>
> That is hard enough.

Finally, remember Al Capone's advice: "You can get much further with a kind word and a gun than you can with a kind word alone."

---

144 Without humour and appropriate playfulness, any sense of "team spirit" is destined to be short-lived.

145 *National Post* (Canada), 16 June 2003.

146 Page 57.

50 ways to make affirmation an extension of who you are

What follows are 50 affirming actions. Think about the past month and check off those that are representative of ones you have used. If the number of checkmarks is a little thin, take it as read that you are not providing the emotional support those around you need. The dilemma: Where self-esteem is low, risk-taking, a willingness to have courageous conversations, and collaboration are stunted. If affirmation is one of your strengths, congratulations! Know that you have uncovered one of the building blocks of a great organization.

1. Start the day out right. Find someone to affirm (even if it's only a smile) or something to make a positive comment about – before you get to work. One of your kids? Someone you don't know but meet regularly on the elevator? Make it a habit.

2. In the typical organization, there are at least five negative comments for every one that is positive. One study suggests the ratio is fifteen to one! And yes, that means you and me. Address the balance by deliberately starting out each business day with three affirmations in your hip pocket. Make sure that you end each day with that pocket empty. Three seems a small number, but over the year it amounts to hundreds of affirming actions. If everyone on your team did the same thing, the impact on self-confidence (and performance) would be dramatic. Cost: nothing. Value: priceless.

3. Reward success by taking the individual(s) with you to a leading-edge workshop or seminar.

4. Reinforce success by writing a handwritten note recognizing the contribution made. Carry around blank postcards (ideally with the organization's values or a relevant symbolic design printed on one side) and discreetly give out with handwritten congratulatory comments.

5. We always have a choice whether to smile or frown. Smile when you come into a meeting. Smile when you start a presentation. Smile when you are asked a

tough question. A smile leads the audience to believe that the speaker is open and optimistic; a frown ... that he/she would rather be someplace else.

6. Do the unexpected. Give out company-ware (a hat, T-shirt) to celebrate when important milestones have been met. Bring movie tickets for the kids. Pay for a session at the spa. Come in early and tie balloons to the employee's chair. Buy someone a tie, arrange for a limo to an event, give him/her a fishing lure, tickets to the opera, send flowers. If the success was achieved as a team, send the team to a spa. Avoid golf! It embarrasses those who don't play and frustrates the heck out of those who do. Note: The traditional "employee of the month" picture that hangs in the entrance hall is a nice idea, but all too quickly becomes just part of the landscape.

7. Contract for a series of planned coaching conversations as a reward for meeting key goals. Challenge the employee to move to the next level.

8. Ask the individual identified above to chair an important meeting.

9. Invite outstanding performers to join a project team where the work the team does will have a real impact on the organization's strategic journey (e.g., change team, selecting external resources to support talent acquisition, designing a career development program.)

10. Ask top performers to attend an important meeting – customer, client, supplier, or vendor – with you.

11. Send a "thank you" card to the employee's home. Phone someone at home and tell them how delighted you are with their performance. Better still, leave a message and know how good they will feel when the message is shared with the family.

12. Put a congratulatory letter in the employee's file. Copy the employee. Copy their team leader.

13. Affirmation can shape relationships. Coach high-potential subordinates in how to coach. This does two things: (1) it affirms the belief that a significant leadership role lies in their future; and (2) it allows you to build a collaborative relationship with each of them.

14. Stop by the successful performer's office unannounced, with a coffee, and spend two minutes affirming their work.

15. Encourage an employee who has made a truly creative contribution to write an article or paper for publication. Work the company's PR department into the equation. Use an external writer if necessary. Apart from the worth of positive reinforcement to the employee, the company's employment value proposition is significantly enhanced.

16. Stop and shake someone's hand. E-mail? Good, if the individual is in another country, but a poor substitute for seeing a warm smile.

17. The comments about e-mails notwithstanding, the Internet has numerous sites with cards, greetings, jingles, and the like. When an appropriate comment is added and when used sparingly, these sites can be a vivid and inexpensive way to say, "job well done."

18. Be interested in what the employee has to say. Put an hour aside where there is no agenda and invite the employees to share their ideas. Suggest that nothing is sacrosanct and anything is possible.

19. Use affirmation to build community. Share market success in real time. For example, make it a tradition that meetings and presentations stop briefly while any new customer sales are shared with participants. Note: With BlackBerry and mobile phones (used during the break), attendees are remarkably well informed.

20. Go out of your way to make positive comments about the individual to their team leader.

21. For truly outstanding performers, give them a blank sheet of paper and ask them to design the nature of their contribution. This should embrace responsibility, accountability, and even scope. You will find that the opportunity is responded to with enthusiasm and integrity.

22. Ask a young, successful employee to mentor a senior executive on the former's area of expertise, e.g., information technology. Note: Reverse mentoring can be a richly rewarding experience for both parties.

23. Recognize the contribution of others in your own success. And don't stick to generalities; be specific regarding the contribution others make. Work positive comments about key individuals into management meetings. Even if the individual isn't there, it will get back to them.

24. Train everyone on the team in storytelling. Start meetings off with storytelling. Encourage each attendee to spend a few moments identifying a recent success. Have the best stories packaged into a storybook. Send copies to customers and suppliers. Put the best stories on the intranet. Keep the stories up-to-date.

25. Organize an "Innovation Olympics." Have employees who have introduced an outstanding level of innovation compete against each other in an organized event. Have a significant prize for the winner. Have innovation shoot-outs between companies within the organization. Make the first prize an all-expenses paid trip to share the value of the innovation with other organizations within the group.

26. When a talented employee stumbles, go out of your way to emphasize the power of learning from mistakes. Share your own less-than-successful ventures.

27. Have a "Wall of Fame." Take a digital picture of the employee targeted for affirmation and briefly identify why, and how, the employee made a difference. Post both the picture and the comments on the Wall of Fame. Tear the wall down at the end of each fiscal year and begin again.

28. Celebrate success. Invite the whole team to a barbeque in the car park after work (a local beauty spot might be even better). Let the team enjoy the time spent together, but also let them know specifically what the performance was that merited the event.

29. Let the successful employee follow the company's product or service into the marketplace. If you make engines for tractors, send the employee to a farm to see how the product is used. If you manufacture software, send the employee to a customer site to see how the product delivers value. If you are a practice leader in a consulting firm and you have a great backroom employee, take him/her on a sales call. Ask for suggestions about product or service improvements when the individual returns. Involvement beyond their normal role will not only reinforce the individual's self-esteem, it will build pride in the organization's product or service.

30. Periodically set aside part of a team meeting, where team members are invited to describe what it is that others on the team do that contributes to the speaker's success. Time set aside for shared affirmation allows positive emotions to be

surfaced, reinforces the value of teamwork, and sets the context for greater mutual support.

31. Listening is just about the best form of affirmation that there is. Following a successful breakthrough, ask the individual responsible to share specifically, and in depth, how it came about. Listen with intensity.

32. Ask a successful employee to teach a class on the topic they excel in. If the organization doesn't have such a class and even if you only run it once ... create one. Be there! Cameo the employee's talent. Make the first invitee the executive responsible for succession planning.

33. Keep your promises both specific and implied. More often than not, trust is about the little things. Be on time. Start meetings on time. End on time. Call people back. Treat everyone on the team the same. Be open to feedback. When people trust you they will be more willing to accept the affirmative statement as coming from someone who cares. Affirmation from someone who cares makes a difference. Affirmation that is seen as self-serving breeds resentment.

34. If you lead a large sales force, and the sales representatives have company vehicles, try this one. Buy five upgraded vehicles (the regular vehicle with a bigger engine, leather seats, and great sound system, for example). Beg, borrow, or buy (company oriented) customized number plates. Allocate the upgraded cars to the top five sales reps for a year. Your sales team will kill to get one of those cars!

35. Confront employees who don't pull their weight. Nothing frustrates talented employees more than having to support those who lack commitment. Nothing affirms a winning attitude more strongly than being part of a team where everyone is playing to win.

36. Reinforce the sightlines between results and opportunity. Follow up outstanding performance with a career discussion. Co-create with the employee a career development plan. Make the plan happen.

37. Take a successful employee to a social event that you know they are good at – even if you are not. Make the celebration about the employee. Allow them to excel. Bowling, anyone?

38. Unceremoniously throw out a performance appraisal process that informs 60% of the workforce that they are "average," "competent," or "meet expectations." Imagery that reinforces a middle-of-the-road mindset, when combined with language that sucks the vitality out of the organization, represents the best thing the competition has going for it. It is also pretty tough to coach someone to be "more average." What's problematic with telling those who met the agreed goals that they were "successful?"

39. Affirm what Susan Scott calls "fierce conversations."[147] Step one: That the leader demonstrate emotional honesty and a willingness to be vulnerable.   Step two: Establish an environment where it is safe to discuss the "non-discussable." Step three: Interrogate reality (in its many guises). Step four: Positively reinforce the actions of those with the courage to initiate such conversations. Step five: Act.

40. Allocate a small number of parking spaces next to the main door for those who have delivered a special result. Award the spaces for a relatively short period of time. The real value lies in the visibility of the affirmation.

41. Advance the salary deadline for truly outstanding performers. Give the employee the agreed salary increase a month early. Be warned, you will probably have to successfully arm-wrestle every single member of the salary administration team to make this happen.

42. Hand the employee an article or a book that in some way reflects the employee's contribution. Better still, use Post-it notes to highlight passages that coincide with how and where the employee excels. It doesn't have to be a business book or article.

43. Reward consistently outstanding front-line employees by awarding additional levels of job security, e.g., they can only be laid off with an extended notice period. Keep the cadre of such employees to less than one-third of the workforce.

44. Consider a "pay it forward" book. It works like this. The team leader buys a hardcover book with blank pages in it. The leader handwrites a heartfelt affirmation statement for someone they believe has recently made an extraordinary contribution.   This first recipient then writes something positive about an individual (or several individuals) who were especially helpful to them. The "pay

---

147 Susan Scott, *Fierce Conversations: Achieving Success at Work & in Life, One Conversation at a Time* (Berkley, 2004).

it forward" book then moves, in turn, to the next individual to be congratulated. After a while, the book has a life of its own.

45. Organize a write-up of the employee's contribution in the company newspaper or intranet site. Whenever possible, accompany it with a photograph.

46. Take an unexpected opportunity (like bumping into a team member at the coffee station) to give positive feedback.

47. Show your respect for the employee's ability by asking for their opinion on issues that are outside their span of responsibilities.

48. With the right person, and delivered in the right way, humour can be a powerful way to reinforce the positive – but be careful! Remember, humour in one culture can come across as something entirely different in another.

49. Make positive comments to a third party; know that the comments will get back to the individual.

50. The suggestions (1–49) reinforce affirmation within the team. Affirmation is no less powerful with customers and suppliers. Indeed, striving for mastery in a sales role without exemplary skills in affirmation is to reach for the impossible dream. Go through the suggested actions and pull out ideas that you can bring to your relationship with key customers.

(See the "Cheering Works!" questionnaire, following.)

Cheering works!

−	+

1 We rarely celebrate success and when we do it's something of an afterthought

`10  9  8  7  6  5  4  3  2  1`

A success isn't truly a success until we have celebrated

`1  2  3  4  5  6  7  8  9  10`

2 Coaching, when it takes place, tends to focus on problems and/ or behavior that has to be "fixed"

`10  9  8  7  6  5  4  3  2  1`

Coaching is alive and well and whenever possible skewed such that the conversation builds on success

`1  2  3  4  5  6  7  8  9  10`

3 The majority of stories that move around the organization focus on problems, issues or mistakes

`10  9  8  7  6  5  4  3  2  1`

When people share a story you can, more or less, guarantee that t will highlight something positive

`1  2  3  4  5  6  7  8  9  10`

4 In-the-moment feedback is dominated by a focus on the things that go wrong

`10  9  8  7  6  5  4  3  2  1`

In-the-moment feedback is aimed at "catching people doing it right"

`1  2  3  4  5  6  7  8  9  10`

5 A not uncommon comment at workshop and meetings is along the lines of, "we understand the need for change, we want to change, but some things here are written in stone"

`10  9  8  7  6  5  4  3  2  1`

The philosophy around here is that we are in charge of our own destiny, and that to lead means confronting, rather than listening to the naysayers, holding courageous conversations and not having to ask for permission to act

`1  2  3  4  5  6  7  8  9  10`

6 When mistakes happen the overwhelming theme is… let's find out who is to blame

`10  9  8  7  6  5  4  3  2  1`

When we stumble the overwhelming theme is… what can we learn from this

`1  2  3  4  5  6  7  8  9  10`

7 When we innovate it's because, "the enemy is at the gate"

`10  9  8  7  6  5  4  3  2  1`

Innovation, x-organization collaboration, and breakthrough thinking are central to our identity

`1  2  3  4  5  6  7  8  9  10`

8 All-too-often, people use the current rules and established practice to explain why we cannot do something

`10  9  8  7  6  5  4  3  2  1`

There is a high comfort level in the organization of pushing back against, reframing and/or changing the rules and practices that "get in the way"

`1  2  3  4  5  6  7  8  9  10`

9 Because the decision-making process is encumbered by over-analysis, an attitude of defensiveness and/or lack of trust of those in the "trenches," we are often slow to act

`10  9  8  7  6  5  4  3  2  1`

Albeit that the decision is based largely on the intuitive feel and experience of those in key roles, when we truly need to be fleet-of-foot we can, and do, act fast

`1  2  3  4  5  6  7  8  9  10`

10 We have great business practices, but people tend to find out about them either by accident or after the optimum point of need has passed

`10  9  8  7  6  5  4  3  2  1`

There is an underlying spirit that drives it, and the business tools are in place to support…sharing best practice

`1  2  3  4  5  6  7  8  9  10`

If affirmation were ever-present in the way leaders around here act, we would:

_____

_____

_____

_____

_____

_____

As an organization, to make "catching people doing it right" central to how leaders think and act, we must:

_____

_____

_____

_____

_____

_____

Starting right now, to ensure that I utilize the power of affirmation even more than I do now, I will:

_____

_____

_____

_____

_____

_____

Part four:
MEASURING
CULTURE

"Hell, there are no rules here.
We're trying to accomplish something."
– *Thomas Alva Edison*

Chapter twelve:
IF YOU CAN'T MEASURE IT, YOU CAN'T MANAGE IT

In an upside-down world

Few, indeed, are those executives who, regardless of country or sector, do not sit down at least once a year to recast the organization's business strategy. The wider **Context**, the **Competition**, the **Customer**, and the **Company**, represent the pivotal four **Cs** of those discussions.[148] In the majority of organizations, a fifth **C** – **Culture** – is either overlooked or given a subordinate role. Pushing culture into the background is not the thinking in organizations that thrive decade after decade. Nor is it the case in those businesses that successfully navigate the turbulent waters of social and economic change. And it is absolutely not the reality in organizations that have an enviable track record in managing aggressive and sustained growth. That being said, there are a good many reasons why culture gets pushed to one side. At the heart of the dilemma, the concern that many executives cannot get past is that, without measurement, culture is too difficult to get your arms around.

The narrative of the trapped mind

"You can't measure culture."

"We see culture as being all about and, for the most part, only about our values."

"Our engagement survey delivers everything we need to know about culture."

"Once we feel we have the strategy right, then we'll look at culture."

"We are in different countries; we have different generational groups; many of our plants and offices are truly multicultural and, because of our aggressive takeover and merger philosophy, our businesses draw on very different histories. We feel the only way we manage that degree of diversity is through a tough posture on financial results. We work on the premise that the rest, "the soft stuff," will, in the end, work itself out."

The rest of the story …

How we learn is who we are.

---

148 This builds on the 3Cs Model developed by Kenichi Ohmae, a business and corporate strategist.

If you can't measure it, you can't manage it

"How we learn is a pervasive part of the way we experience life."

The case was made in Chapter three: If you're not managing your culture, someone else is. This speaks to clarity and inspiration from the top team in general and the chief executive, in particular; understanding culture as a system; bringing the culture conversation into the middle of the organization; and the need to map (measure) the change demanded. Take it as a given: Without measurement, culture is destined to remain an abstract, slippery, difficult-to-get-at project on the human resource department's to-do list.

Even assuming the above are in place, six additional issues quickly derail culture initiatives:

1. Failure to keep the change agenda simple – middle managers tune out.

2. Lack of a golden thread linking all of the parts – the work being undertaken comes across as a series of standalone, disconnected, confusing actions.

3. When those in pivotal leadership positions fail to model the new behaviour demanded – if those at the top don't go out of their way to convince people that they are committed to the new order of things, little will change.

4. Little attention given to the new skills needed – It's not enough to urge employees to behave differently; those involved have to be equipped to behave differently.

5. An overall approach that (ironically) reinforces the very culture those leading the charge want to change (i.e., to the extent possible, the process being employed to bring about the change should model the culture the organization is seeking to create). When the culture challenge is to reduce the speed to market, for example, it helps not at all that the process used to bring that about is itself slow and ponderous.

6. When there is lack of clarity around the culture demanded, what we don't know inevitably becomes overwhelmed by what we do know. Put another way, when what isn't working today becomes the focus of attention rather than the outcome sought, gridlock is assured.

The account that follows explores the thinking behind a simple but penetrating measurement of an organization's cultural journey. Building on research by the author and first published in the 1990s, the **"Culture Work-Up"** that follows draws on the time-established relationship between learning and culture.

The rationale: By examining dominant learning themes within the organization and then evaluating those insights against "the emerging business needs," we build a unique culture assessment of (1) how things happen today, and (2) where the organization needs (not wants) to be at a prescribed date in the future.

The Culture Work-Up measures culture across sixteen key dimensions. Teams going through the work-up (in some instances an individual[149]) are presented with a range of distinctive cultural perspectives. What emerges – through dialogue, challenge, and forced choice – is a robust map of the current and emerging cultural terrain.

To explore learning as culture, to get the most out of the Culture Work-Up that follows, it is helpful to first understand the following:

1. How we learn is who we are.

How we learn is a pervasive part of the way we experience life. As a simple example, think about a young child with a new toy. Out of the box the toy, a small car for example, is greeted with an easy to anticipate response: The child pushes it along, much as they have seen a real car moving (and as the designer intended). We can refer to this as **simple learning.**

> *How we learn is a pervasive part of the way we experience life.*

Literally, within minutes, however, the child becomes tired of this undemanding simulation. The response: What else can the "car" do? Will it still work if it has no wheels? What happens if it crashes into the kitchen door? Will the box it came in make a good garage? We can describe this as **learning how to learn.**

Now, as any parent knows too well, before long the toy itself is either broken or pushed aside. Does that mean that the derived learning (from the toy car) comes to an end? No, even though no longer physically present, the learning stimulated by the car is revisited in imagination and play. We can call this **learning how to learn, limited only by the imagination of the learner.**

---

149 In support of a key leader moving into a new role or a new organization.

The hypothesis being presented is that there are three distinct levels of learning: (1) simple learning, (2) learning how to learn (but where you need something concrete to stimulate the learning process), and (3) learning how to learn – limited only by imagination. I refer to these learning plateaus as **Territory 1**, **Territory 2**, and **Territory 3**, respectively.

These three approaches to learning are repeated in virtually every aspect of our lives. Take art, for example. For the viewer, a classical painting such as a Canaletto,[150] who painted to the best of his ability exactly what he saw, represents simple learning. Impressionist art (e.g., Gauguin), however, demands that the viewer interpret the artist's intent (learning how to learn).[151] In Modern art (e.g., Picasso), the interpretation rests solely with the viewer's imagination (it means what you want it to mean).[152]

Moving on to a more perplexing topic, we land on an aspect of learning that troubles even the most secure of nations: terrorism. Traditional military training focuses on stripping out individual differences (get a haircut, put on the uniform, say hello to the nice drill sergeant, and keep your head down while we shoot live ammunition at you); and conditioning aimed at ensuring the recruit will act in a preordained way, operate within the established structure and, above all else, follow orders. After all, it's really all about getting the "grunts"[153] up the hill. This can be defined as **Simple learning.**

The speed of modern warfare, combined with the technology at hand means that today's soldier has to be able to interpret what is happening around them, factor in different potential scenarios, take into account the rules of engagement and then, in real time, act accordingly. In most instances, there simply isn't time to wait for orders. This can be defined as **Learning how to learn.**

Meanwhile, radical terrorist groups have few, if any, boundaries that limit how they are organized and operate. The outcome: Terrorist cells have the ability to continuously morph into entirely new forms based on the assumed response of "the enemy"[154] and the politics of the day. This can be defined as **Learning how to learn, limited only by the imagination of the learner.**[155]

---

150 Canaletto's paintings depict life in Venice in the eighteenth century.

151 It is interesting to note that Impressionist art emerged in France relatively shortly after photography was discovered. Louis-Jacques-Mandé Daguerre first displayed his "photographs" to members of the French Académie des Sciences on 7 January 1839. The first exhibition of Impressionist art took place in Paris in 1874.

152 This is reflected in a quote from artist Jackson Pollock (1912–1956): "It [abstract art] should be enjoyed just as music is enjoyed – after a while you may like it or you may not."

153 Slang for infantry.

154 Although they have the most advanced weapon systems in the world, American and British forces went into Iraq with vehicles ill-equipped to deal with improvised explosive devices (IEDs) – roadside bombs that insurgents build from cast-off artillery shells.

155 In June 2008, the Obama administration dropped the term "global war on terror" as too "limiting." The term "war" portrayed a traditional conflict (and by implication, approach) between nation-states.

2. "Yes we can" measure culture.

In the recent past, a good deal of fuss was made of "the learning organization." Sadly, few of the ideas presented were actually about **learning.** The result: A potentially insightful way to think about the modern organization became devalued to the point where, today, the term is little more than a catch-all for a hodgepodge of consulting, training, and talent management products.

And yet, how well the organization (e.g., people, systems, processes) responds to a rapidly changing business and economic environment (i.e., accesses past learning and acquires new ways to act) is truly an invaluable piece of the competitive puzzle. After all, survival isn't about being the biggest or the best – it's about how quickly those who shape possibility can adapt; it's ultimately about how the organization learns.

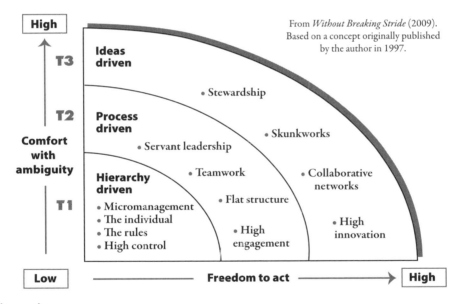

From *Without Breaking Stride* (2009). Based on a concept originally published by the author in 1997.

Figure nine

Enter stage left: Territory1 (T1), Territory 2 (T2), and Territory 3 (T3). Figure nine outlines the three basic learning archetypes described earlier, interpreted as three quite different organizational forms. Each archetype (e.g., T1) clusters the dominant assumptions (e.g., micromanagement, the individual, the rules, high control) around the culture that is reinforced and replicated.[156]

---

156 This work is referenced in *New Role, New Reality* (2000); *Leaders Must Lead!* (2003); and *Without Breaking Stride* (2009).

One way in which these three archetypes surface is found in the degree of freedom to act. In a traditional, hierarchical business (retail banking, mining, manufacturing, automotive, retail, government)[157] there is, taken overall, relatively little room for employees to display personal discretion (T1). In businesses that exhibit a flexible approach to sales and marketing and where the product or service is high-value-added (selling complex systems, large engineering projects, established consulting firms), there is a high degree of freedom to act (T2). Meanwhile, in organizations that compete largely on the depth and quality of their intellectual property (the on-line Linux community, new product development in high-tech, the creative teams in an advertising agency, managing talent in the entertainment business, an art house that creates breakthrough design) people enjoy, of necessity, considerable freedom to act (T3).

> *In terms of collaboration and spontaneity, think "flash mob" when describing a T3 way to work.*

The accelerated growth of T3 organization forms is, in no small measure, a reflection of breakthrough technology that has enabled collaborative networks in their many forms to flourish. T3 organizations go by names like Wikipedia, Napster, the Human Genome Project, YouTube, Second Life, Flickr, ICICI Bank, Monster, InnoCentive, and CollabNet. In terms of collaboration and spontaneity, think "flash mob" when describing a T3 way to work.[158]

T1 organizations were designed to produce and deliver goods and services. People were there essentially to mind the machines – the philosophy being: "If we make it, they will come." T2 organizations were designed to support the customer's emerging needs. Developing human potential, although a significant investment, inevitably taking a back seat to process efficiency. T3 organizations are designed around people. Their capacity to deliver innovation lies in the fact that they reflect a way to come together that, given a choice, is exactly how people would choose to work.

T1 organizations are all about "power-over." T2 organizations essentially reflect a "power-with" mindset. T3 organizations are based on a "power-to" belief system. In a world where the war for talent is back on, where demographics put tomorrow's employee in the driving seat, and where a new, highly independent generation is entering the workforce, it's not much of a mystery as to which organizational forms are

---

157 The examples given here are sweeping generalities only. Individual organizations may not fall under the cultural archetypes described.

158 A flash mob is a large group of people who seem to spontaneously converge in a public place, put on a coordinated group performance such as a song, a dance, or a demonstration, then just as "spontaneously" melt back into the crowd. It's all prearranged and launched using mobile phones and social media networking.

going to have the greatest challenge in hiring and retaining top talent. Indeed, within what type of organization would you recommend your bright and articulate twenty-year-old son or daughter develop their career?

Although appropriately dominated by one "territory,"[159] many organizations deliberately embrace all three. 3M is a case in point. Manufacturing is T1; the traditional approach to R&D is T2; but that part of their work time (15%) that engineers are given license to work independently is T3.[160]

3. My homework ate the dog.

The first 80 years of the last century were all about the management of money, men, materials, and machines (data/information). The most recent 25 years or so have focused on leading people (knowledge). From here on in, success will be all about creating the right context such that people can lead themselves (knowledge of knowledge).

When unpredictable scenarios become the norm, the wider cultural implications of T1, T2, and T3 take on even greater importance. For example:

> *From here on in, success will be all about creating the right context such that people can lead themselves.*

> The language, speed of action, propensity for risk, and need for comfort with ambiguity changes significantly in T1, T2, and T3.

> What it means to be a team, the way teams are expected to work together and the role played by the informal organization changes dramatically as one moves across T1, T2, and T3.

> If the leadership role entails working across a large complex business, effectiveness means being personally agile enough to embrace, as needed, T1, T2, and T3. Leadership success thus means having a "tool bag" of systems, processes, structures, and approaches to be used as needed.[161] By way of example, this implies an approach to talent acquisition,[162] succession management, compensation, and/or coaching that differs in T1, T2, and T3. The wider implication: We need to rethink the notion of leadership "style" and start referring to "styles." That does not mean that

---

159 "Managing culture" means orchestrating both "sameness" and diversity. Even in complex organizations where they deliberately embrace T1, T2, and T3, there is a need to define an overarching, cultural anchor point (along the T1–T2–T3 continuum): a single cultural hinge (business identity/story) around which the various sub-cultures pivot.

160 In some organizations (e.g., Lockheed Martin's Advanced Development Programs), this mode of working is often referred to as "skunkworks." This term is widely used to describe a group given a high degree of autonomy.

161 This builds on an idea first proposed by the late Peter Drucker.

162 The overwhelming evidence is that very few organizations have a disciplined way to measure "tomorrow's culture" as a key dimension of "fit" in the hiring process.

the "agility" being described equates to loss of integrity or pulling back on personal values.

> Key account management, partnership, outsourcing and collaboration decisions that don't factor-in the potential conflict drawn out of working across different learning/cultural platforms (archetypes) are destined to be both conflict-ridden and ever-frustrating for everyone involved.

> In that roughly two-thirds of all mergers and acquisitions fail, and that the root cause of that shortfall more often than not lies with culture, exploring "fit" through the T1, T2, T3 lens has the potential to (1) better inform the decision-making process, (2) add significantly to the integration strategy options, and (3) provide insight to key executives regarding personal integration into the new entity. [163]

A number of businesses have introduced what can best be described as "parallel structures" into their way of working. Automotive assembly is dominated by (1) the speed of the assembly process (how fast the line moves), (2) the length of time it takes to complete each operation (very limited), and (3) the ease of access to new parts (Just-in-Time, or JIT). Following time-given tradition, the worker is an extension of the "machine." Even the movement of operators between assembly stations does little to change what is, essentially, a T1 way to work. In the off hours (evening and weekends), however, leading-edge employers bring operators together in teams to work on (improve and change) those same processes that dominate their every movement during the day (T2). In inviting those same front-line workers to play a role in developing the next generation of vehicles, by tapping into the organization's collective knowledge, a parallel T3 platform emerges. Technology, open source systems, new ways to enable organization-wide collaboration, and the capacity to turn know-how into knowledge have the potential to not merely change culture, but to transform it.

While the previous example underscores that there are ways to "enrich" even the most repetitive tasks, there is also clear evidence that there are times when a T1 way to work is the most efficient and productive approach – whether it be running a start-up software team in Russia, a textile factory in Vietnam, or a call centre in Mumbai.[164] A high number of temporary workers or a high percentage of the workforce who struggle with a common national language also point to a T1 approach.

---

163 Organizations use terms such as "merger" and "acquisition," but the true outcome is that a new entity inevitably emerges – ideally, one that builds on the best of both organizations.

164 Short term expediency may rule, but in the examples given there is no intent to suggest any lack of capacity to move to a T2 or even a T3 Platform.

4. Would the last person to leave please turn the lights off?

The dilemma: A deeply embedded T1 culture carries high "knock-on" costs. Writ large in that regard: (1) lack of innovation; (2) the problem of hiring and retaining Gen Y (and younger) employees; (3) difficulty in building a strong service ethos; (4) a vibrant, but not necessarily supportive grapevine; and (5) because the workers have little influence over how the work is carried out, wide-scale pushback to new ways to operate.

A business culture built on and dominated by T1 work also has long-term impact on the economy overall. The average worker in highly developed countries (such as Canada, the United States, the UK, France, Germany, Australia) joins the workforce having benefited from a very expensive education. From the wider societal perspective, "dumbed-down" (T1) work represents a poor return on that investment. And considering the wages paid for that (simple) work in Europe and North America, it also often amounts to a questionable investment on the part of the employer. Take it as a given, therefore: T1 work will continue to flow to where it makes most economic sense – the "developing" countries of the world. [165]

The challenge: Unless as a society we can rekindle the spirit of innovation that made us extraordinarily successful; unless we find new ways to access the deep well of unharnessed creative energy available; unless we move beyond cultural drift; unless we, literally, reinvent this thing we call "an organization" – the best of times lie in our past.

> *Technology, open source systems, new ways to enable organization-wide collaboration, and the capacity to turn know-how into knowledge have the potential to not merely change culture, but to transform it.*

Take the time to work through the Culture Work-Up that follows. Remember, if you're not managing your culture, someone else is! The best place to start: defining today's culture and assessing that insight against the culture you need moving forward. Remember: If you can't measure it, you can't manage it.

---

165 The Indian conglomerate Tata Group, acquired Jaguar, Rover, Range Rover, and Daimler in March 2008.

As an organization, if we had a robust way to measure culture, we would:

_____

_____

_____

_____

_____

_____

To introduce a meaningful culture measurement tool, we need to:

_____

_____

_____

_____

_____

_____

Starting now, to ensure that we measure both today's culture and the culture we need to succeed, the role I will play is:

_____

_____

_____

_____

_____

_____

THE CULTURE "WORK-UP"

Where is Your Culture Today? Where Do You Need It to be Tomorrow?

What is culture?

Culture isn't a series of stand alone activities – it's a system. It's a fluid, collective way to be that changes whether those who are responsible for defining "how we need things to happen around here" want it to or not. It's a transmitted pattern of meaning framed by where the organization has been and what it has the potential to become.

Culture is a multi-faceted hologram where every element carries a blueprint of the whole; a shared story that follows a simple rule – change any part and you impact the whole.   To that end, "harmony" (managing the symbiotic relationship between all of the parts) trumps "alignment" (addressing one element at a time). There is a further challenge: leaders are invariably more comfortable initiating actions that drive the culture in a new direction, e.g., strategy, structure, brand, performance management, (the culture drivers) than they are in "working" the elements that, if not addressed, reinforce and continue to reinforce the status quo, e.g., symbolism, values, story, metaphor, language, risk, speed of action (the culture anchors).

Culture thrives at different levels. On the surface is that which can be observed: the formal structure; visible artifacts; how people dress; the level of courtesy; the degree of interpersonal intimacy; the use of humour; whether meetings start on time; how customers' concerns are dealt with; the nature and role of humour; and the tolerance for candour.

What is still observable, but a little more subtle to "read" are: what gets measured; the speed at which things happen; the extent to which the organization is driven from the outside-in or the inside-out; who has power/status and how that power is used (or not); what people are proud of; how and in what ways the customer's voice is heard; group norms; the rules that are open to "interpretation"; support for issues such as work-life balance; how the performance management process actually works; espoused values; and the real role (as opposed to the desired role) of middle managers.

Going deeper, and here one has to dig to understand what is implied, are cultural signals that reveal: stakeholder influence i.e., shareholder, customer, employee and community impact on priorities; what it means to be a successful leader (e.g., who gets promoted and who is struggling); the nature and degree of employee engagement; who's who in the informal organization; what's going to get you into trouble in dealing with the outside world; the sub-text behind the language used; the tolerance (or lack of) for ambiguity; what "freedom to act" implies; assumptions about boundaries and common space; the degree of risk that is acceptable; how difficult decisions get made; the transformative role of technology; how new ideas gain traction; and what collaboration means in practice.

Moving down to the bedrock of culture we come to: the founder's legacy; symbolism; ritual; myths; root metaphors; the dominant meta story; deeply held beliefs; the ingrained values (as opposed to the espoused values); default habits of thinking; shared mindset; common identity; how people learn; and the organization's relationship with the planet.

The value of the work-up

The reason to go through the culture work-up is to answer the overriding question, "What do we need to do differently today, to achieve outstanding business results tomorrow?" Other essential benefits include:

> By defining where we are and where we need to be, we have an invaluable backdrop for all coaching discussions, a central plank in the recruitment process, and a priceless way to shape the conversation around strategy.

> By exposing the Board of Directors to the culture work-up, the role the Board plays in talent management, compensation, and decisions regarding succession is given a solid foundation.

> By making the culture journey central to the ongoing conversation with middle managers, their potential contribution can be better surfaced and thus understood.

> By flexing training and development investment against the culture we need around here, return on investment is significantly improved.

> By weaving a cultural assessment into the executive integration process, the dominant reason why new leaders fail becomes imminently manageable.

> By going through the culture work-up prior to, and as part of, the acquisition decision, the reason why most acquisitions fail can be better avoided. For "acquisition" read "business integration."

Assessing culture

The assessment that follows looks at culture through a learning lens. A simple but profound way to describe culture, the unique "work-up" that is produced builds on the following assumptions:

> Set against the unfolding business context, how the organization learns is a simple and compelling measure of today's culture and the culture we need.

> There are three distinctly different plateaus of learning: (1) simple learning; (2) learning how to learn; and (3) learning how to learn, limited only by the imagination of the learner.

> Although most organizations have more than one culture, there is a dominant culture that, like the hinge on a garden gate, everything else is anchored to. Speed, movement, and degree of turbulence may differ but there is always an eye at the centre of every storm. Were this not so, no organization would be able to operate in any form other than as a portfolio of separate businesses. This is not to say that going through the culture work-up with different sectors, divisions and/or parts of the business in mind is not extraordinarily useful.

The work-up

Starting with Leadership (#1) and ending with Speed of Response (#16), the culture work-up looks at sixteen distinct dimensions of culture. Each dimension is presented as a cultural continuum (1-10) and is supported by three graduated statements, e.g., Bosship, Servant leadership, Stewardship.

Go through the work-up one dimension at a time. Determine where your organization (or that part of the business you are focusing on) is today, and then establish (for each dimension) where, moving forward, you need to be. To avoid confusion, when you score the work-up, use a symbol that differentiates where you are today from where you need to be. The example given uses a circle and a check mark.

The time-span looking forward depends on the business sector you are in. In a fast moving sector, in a business start-up, or turnaround, three years or even less may be appropriate. In a traditional business, five years is a good default option. How far you look into the future is a matter of judgement. Consider doing the work-up a second time. The first time use a three-to-five-year time horizon. The second assessment, seven to ten years out.

Before going through the work-up, reflect on the unfolding business context. Think about upcoming changes in technology, the economic scenarios your business is facing, the demographic picture, the challenge of attracting and retaining a new generation, the competitive arena, the political reality, and the talent available in-house.

In framing the culture, be pragmatic. Think about what you need and can become – not, in a perfect world, what you would like to become. Weave in the reality of the emerging context but make the future you define real, not aspirational. If in doubt, always return to the question, What do we need to do to deliver tomorrow's business performance?

In completing the work-up, your assessment should be guided by the three culture statements, but can fall anywhere along the 1-10 continuum. For example, if in looking at Leadership you feel that Bosship describes exactly where you are today, your assessment would be "2." If you feel you are starting to creep beyond that, your assessment might well be "3." If, however, you believe you are at the early stages of Servant leadership, you would probably want to assess the current situation as a "4." Use the same thinking when describing the culture you need (not want). Anything defined as a "9" or "10" would be pushing the culture you have in mind to the extreme. On the other end of the scale, if, for example, Bosship has a hard edge, you might want to assess it as a "1."

There is a natural tendency to see a low score as bad and a high score as good. Indeed, in attracting and retaining talent, in the push for innovation, to enhance the speed at which things happen, a low score will hold the organization back. On the other hand, there are situations where "Bosship," or "Tell me how to do it," for example, are very appropriate, e.g., a workforce dominated by temporary employees and where the turnover is high. Note: if your organization makes explosives, then "Learning as play" may not be a good idea.

You can complete the assessment on your own, or with your team. The latter, in that dialogue around the assessment draws out the thinking and feelings that support each individual's assessment, is especially valuable.

1. LEADERSHIP

BOSSHIP	SERVANT LEADERSHIP	STEWARDSHIP
Leadership is dominated by a command and control approach. Strong emphasis on established practice, formal authority, rules and policies.	Trust, listening, humility, caring and authenticity describe what it means to be a successful leader. To lead is to put the employee first.	The impact of decisions on the wider community is seen (literally) as important, and receives as much attention, as meeting the needs of customers and/or shareholders.

1   2   3   4   5   6   7   8   9   10

2. STRUCTURE

HIERARCHY	BEYOND HIERARCHY	VIRTUAL
Our current structure is dominated by the traditional hierarchy. The silos rule!	We have toppled the pyramid and created an organization where end-to-end processes define our structure.	We have no permanent structure; teams are constantly forming and reforming. Innovation is a way of life.

1   2   3   4   5   6   7   8   9   10

3. KNOWLEDGE MANAGEMENT

"KNOW-HOW"	KNOWLEDGE	KNOWLEDGE OF KNOWLEDGE
For the most part knowledge lies with key individuals. When they leave, much of what they know goes with them.	We successfully codify know-how and store winning and proven practice in easy-to-access knowledge banks.	In the sector we are in, we are renowned for our ability to find new ways to create, share and disseminate new knowledge.

1   2   3   4   5   6   7   8   9   10

4. LEARNING MINDSET

TELL ME HOW TO DO IT	EXPLORATION	LEARNING AS PLAY
Learning is largely through instruction. The employee is told what to do and expected to get on with it. If they get stuck, the answer will be provided.	Learning is dominated by a willingness to ask new questions, exploring best practice, and a general theme of team members coaching each other.	The majority of our employees have 15% or more of his/her time that is totally unstructured. This is space set aside to invent, innovate and pursue new ideas.

1   2   3   4   5   6   7   8   9   10

5. TEAMWORK

"MARCHING BAND"	"STRING QUARTET"	"JAZZ BAND"
Limited repertoire of music. Teams expected to follow the leader. The leader's message: "Stay in line and follow me."	Aggressive, committed and highly disciplined. The skills of each performer blend together. It's difficult to know who has taken the lead.	Agile, quick to improvise, we constantly break new ground. Moving beyond what has gone before is a given. Who leads the team is a reflection of the opportunity on hand.

1   2   3   4   5   6   7   8   9   10

6. WHAT PEOPLE COMPLAIN ABOUT

MANAGEMENT	KEY PROCESSES	SCOPE OF MY ROLE
"Management doesn't really understand the problems we have and/or the way things get done around here."	We need to be simpler in everything we do, work harder at collaboration and re-engage middle management.	The degree of freedom, the amount of risk, the push to continuously learn and the need to come up with ideas is stimulating, but stressful.

1   2   3   4   5   6   7   8   9   10

7. COMPENSATION

INDIVIDUAL REWARDS	THE "WHAT" AND THE "HOW"	BUILDING COMMUNITY
Compensation and performance feedback are largely skewed towards (1) individual contribution; (2) the results achieved.	Our performance management approach emphasizes team success. It also balances the results (50%) with the behaviour that drives results (50%).	Issues such as social responsibility, fair treatment of off-shore suppliers, sustainability, diversity, and work-life balance play a central role in our reward system.

1   2   3   4   5   6   7   8   9   10

8. INTEGRATION

FIGURE IT OUT	WITHOUT BREAKING STRIDE	CREATE THE ROLE
Apart from the traditional induction program, new hires, for the most part, are expected to figure it out.	Those moving into new roles have an array of leading-edge tools, including: in-house mentoring, masterful coaching, and a means to assess team fit.	New employees first find out about the business. They then define/create and move into the role where they believe they can make the greatest contribution.

1   2   3   4   5   6   7   8   9   10

9. CUSTOMER ORIENTATION

PRODUCT/SERVICE DRIVEN	CUSTOMER-FACING	CREATE THE MARKET
We have a great product/service. Our philosophy is, "If we make it, they will come." Sales theme: "This is why you should buy from us."	We strive to become ever-better at understanding the customer's emerging needs. Sales theme: "How can we make your business/life better?"	Success is developing unique products and services that the customer doesn't know they need. Sales theme: "We will change how your business does business (lifestyle)."

1   2   3   4   5   6   7   8   9   10

10. CULTIVATE THE GRAPEVINE

STORIES	STORYTELLERS	STORYTELLING
We don't have a specific focus on managing the grapevine. We abound with stories, however. The dilemma: most of them are negative.	Storytelling is central to our leadership development agenda. The vast majority of our managers and leaders regularly share positive stories.	We are the definitive storytelling organization. We even have a team whose exclusive role is to collect, hone and propagate stories across the organization.

1   2   3   4   5   6   7   8   9   10

11. TALENT MANAGEMENT

THE INTERVIEW	TEAM FIT	CULTURE FIT
When we bring someone new on board, the issue of "fit" is heavily dependent upon the traditional interview process.	In defining fit we draw on role-specific competencies, a comprehensive performance scorecard, an assessment of team effectiveness and forensic reference checking.	We hire and promote people with tomorrow's culture in mind. To that end, we have robust tools to measure the culture we have – and the culture we need.

1   2   3   4   5   6   7   8   9   10

12. ENGINE OF GROWTH

SHORT-TERM	BUILDING FOR TOMORROW	BEYOND ONE-SIZE-FITS-ALL
Overall, we tend to be driven by relatively short-term financial targets. If we meet the goals, we have been successful.	Growth means growing our people. True excellence in hiring, best-in-class leadership development, and mastery in coaching define who we are.	Our ability to attract and retain the best is based on a culture where **every** employee has the opportunity to negotiate a **unique** employment contract.

1   2   3   4   5   6   7   8   9   10

13. CANDOUR

SOME PLACES, SOMETIMES	GENERALLY, ALIVE AND WELL	INGRAINED IN OUR VALUES
Problems that have to be fixed **"now,"** lack of trust, and/or political games playing mean, as often as not, we duck the tough conversation.	Intolerance of self-serving behaviour, openness, and a willingness for leaders to be vulnerable mean that "candour" is how the majority of teams operate.	Candour is ingrained in our values. It's simply who we are. Leaders who lack this quality either address that behaviour quickly or exit the organization.
1 2 3	4 5 6 7	8 9 10

14. APPROACH TO CHANGE

ONE MORE PROJECT!	CHANGE NEVER ENDS	A CHANGE-READY CULTURE
A problem-solving mindset, assumptions about resistance to change and a focus on overcoming barriers to change best describe our approach.	A compelling purpose, openness, involving people and a recognition that little happens without inspirational leadership define our thinking.	Our whole approach is to build an agile, change-ready organization. Although we build a range of strategic scenarios, culture has primacy over strategy.
1 2 3	4 5 6 7	8 9 10

15. SPIRIT OF AFFIRMATION

"GOTCHA!"	EMPHASIZE THE POSITIVE	INGRAINED IN OUR DNA
When things go wrong, there is a tendency to look for who to blame.	Our overriding practice is to "catch people doing it right." This theme is emphasized in ongoing dialogue, in-the-moment feedback, and at every meeting (extrinsic).	The freedom to make decisions, the scope of people's roles and time deliberately set aside for team and individual reflection means our culture is self-affirming (intrinsic).
1 2 3	4 5 6 7	8 9 10

16. SPEED OF RESPONSE

WE WILL GET TO IT	FLEET-OF-FOOT	BURN TO EARN
The policies, procedures, processes and our risk-averse culture mean we take longer to do things than is ideal.	Moving faster is a business priority. We work hard to simplify processes. There are also times when we eschew analysis and make intuitive decisions.	Speed is who we are. What the competition can't respond to is our history of being first; our capacity to change gears when needed; and our mindset around being fast.
1 2 3	4 5 6 7	8 9 10

Culture work-up

Organization: Example   Date ....

HOW THINGS HAPPEN AROUND HERE	TERRITORY 1	TERRITORY 2	TERRITORY 3
1. LEADERSHIP	Bosship 1 2● 3	Servant leadership 4 5 ✔ 7	Stewardship 8 9 10
2. STRUCTURE	Hierarchy 1● 2 3	Beyond hierarchy 4 5 ✔ 7	Virtual 8 9 10
3. KNOWLEDGE MANAGEMENT	"Know-how" 1 2● 3	Knowledge 4 5 ✔ 7	Knowledge of knowledge 8 9 10
4. LEARNING MINDSET	Tell me how to do it! 1 2 3	Exploration ● 5 6 7	Learning as play 8 ✔ 9 10
5. TEAMWORK	"Marching band" 1 2 ● 4	"String quartet" 5 ✔ 6 7	"Jazz band" 8 9 10
6. WHAT PEOPLE COMPLAIN ABOUT	Management 1 2 3	Key processes 4● 5 6 ✔	Scope of my role 8 9 10
7. COMPENSATION	Individual rewards 1 2● 3	The "what" and the "how" 4 5 6 7	Building community ✔ 9 10
8. INTEGRATION	Figure it out 1 2 3	Without breaking stride ● 5 6 ✔ 7	Create the role 8 9 10
9. CUSTOMER ORIENTATION	Product/service driven 1 2 3●	Customer-facing 4 5 6 ✔ 7	Create the market 8 9 10
10. CULTIVATE THE "GRAPEVINE"	Stories 1 2 3●	Storytellers 4 5✔ 6 7	Storytelling 8 9 10
11. TALENT MANAGEMENT	The interview 1 2 3	Team fit ● 5 6 7	Culture fit 8 ✔ 9 10
12. ENGINE OF GROWTH	Short-term 1 2 3	Building for tomorrow 4● 5 6 ✔	Beyond one-size-fits-all 8 9 10
13. CANDOUR	Some places, sometimes 1 2 3● 4	Generally, alive and well 5 6 7	Ingrained in our values ✔ 8 9 10
14. APPROACH TO CHANGE	One more project! 1 2● 3	Change never ends 4 5 ✔ 6 7	A change-ready culture 8 9 10
15. SPIRIT OF AFFIRMATION	"Gotcha!" 1 2● 3	Emphasize the positive 4 5 6 7	Ingrained in our DNA ✔ 8 9 10
16. SPEED OF RESPONSE	We will get to it 1 2 3● 4	Fleet-of-foot 5 6 ✔ 7	Burn to earn 8 9 10

● Where we are today?   ✔ Based on the emerging marketplace, where we need to be?

Culture work-up

Organization: .... Date ....

HOW THINGS HAPPEN AROUND HERE	TERRITORY 1				TERRITORY 2				TERRITORY 3		
1. LEADERSHIP	Bosship				Servant leadership				Stewardship		
	1	2	3		4	5	6	7	8	9	10
2. STRUCTURE	Hierarchy				Beyond hierarchy				Virtual		
	1	2	3		4	5	6	7	8	9	10
3. KNOWLEDGE MANAGEMENT	"Know-how"				Knowledge				Knowledge of knowledge		
	1	2	3		4	5	6	7	8	9	10
4. LEARNING MINDSET	Tell me how to do it!				Exploration				Learning as play		
	1	2	3		4	5	6	7	8	9	10
5. TEAMWORK	"Marching band"				"String quartet"				"Jazz band"		
	1	2	3		4	5	6	7	8	9	10
6. WHAT PEOPLE COMPLAIN ABOUT	Management				Key processes				Scope of my role		
	1	2	3		4	5	6	7	8	9	10
7. COMPENSATION	Individual rewards				The "what" and the "how"				Building community		
	1	2	3		4	5	6	7	8	9	10
8. INTEGRATION	Figure it out				Without breaking stride				Create the role		
	1	2	3		4	5	6	7	8	9	10
9. CUSTOMER ORIENTATION	Product/service driven				Customer-facing				Create the market		
	1	2	3		4	5	6	7	8	9	10
10. CULTIVATE THE "GRAPEVINE"	Stories				Storytellers				Storytelling		
	1	2	3		4	5	6	7	8	9	10
11. TALENT MANAGEMENT	The interview				Team fit				Culture fit		
	1	2	3		4	5	6	7	8	9	10
12. ENGINE OF GROWTH	Short-term				Building for tomorrow				Beyond one-size-fits-all		
	1	2	3		4	5	6	7	8	9	10
13. CANDOUR	Some places, sometimes				Generally, alive and well				Ingrained in our values		
	1	2	3		4	5	6	7	8	9	10
14. APPROACH TO CHANGE	One more project!				Change never ends				A change-ready culture		
	1	2	3		4	5	6	7	8	9	10
15. SPIRIT OF AFFIRMATION	"Gotcha!"				Emphasize the positive				Ingrained in our DNA		
	1	2	3		4	5	6	7	8	9	10
16. SPEED OF RESPONSE	We will get to it				Fleet-of-foot				Burn to earn		
	1	2	3		4	5	6	7	8	9	10

● Where we are today?   ✓ Based on the emerging marketplace, where we need to be?

Interpreting your assessment

When you have been through the work-up, what should you be looking for?

1. Be conscious of the overall pattern or theme. That is to say, if the shift in culture demanded overall is from T1 to T2 or from T2 to T3, this amounts to more than just one more change initiative. What is being described is a fundamental shift in the way the business does business – an entirely different, underpinning mindset.

2. Look for fundamental gaps between today's culture and the culture you perceive you need to drive tomorrow's performance. For example, if innovation, freedom to act and organization agility describe the future and yet today's leadership approach is dominated by hierarchy and bosship, redefining what it means to be a successful leader becomes an organizational imperative.

3. If, in any key dimension, the culture shift being suggested is significant, look around you and consider: do those in key leadership roles have the capacity and imagination needed to make this happen?

4. Does the work-up suggest a jump from T1 to T3 in any single dimension? Unless you are prepared to metaphorically blow the organization up and start again, this is stretching the bounds of possibility.

5. If you're sitting at the top of the organization, you need to validate your assessment, especially regarding what you perceive to be today's culture, with other groups inside (possibly outside) the organization. Involve middle managers, employees who interface with the customers and/or those deemed high-potential in this dialogue.

6. Does everyone on the team agree on the scope of change implied? Have you agreed on a time-frame that is realistic?

7. Review the work-up and build agreement around:

    (1) What needs to be done.

    (2) Who is going to do it.

    (3) Whose support is needed.

    (4) Developing new relationships and/or fixing old ones.

    (5) Delivery.

    (6) Developing the leaders involved.

    (7) When and how reflection is going to be part of the process.

8. What complementary changes to the culture (from what to what) – not embraced by the work-up – do you also need to work on?

215

Moving the culture forward

What could you do that you're not doing now that would allow your team/organization to better "manage" your culture?

_____

_____

_____

_____

_____

_____

In terms of the future you need to create, what concerns you most about what the assessment tells you?

_____

_____

_____

_____

_____

_____

_____

What's already happening within the organization that you can build on?

_____

_____

_____

_____

_____

_____

Moving the culture forward *(continued)*

What other organizations, insofar as culture is concerned, could you learn from? How are you going to make that happen?

_____

_____

_____

_____

_____

_____

Beginnings start with endings. What does the organization/your team need to let go of?

How soon are you going start?

_____

_____

_____

_____

_____

_____

If you were going to personally do one thing differently on Monday, what would it be?

_____

_____

_____

_____

_____

_____

John has a wealth of business experience as a senior executive on both sides of the Atlantic. As a consultant, he has worked in twenty-five countries for clients that are household names.

He holds a doctoral degree in Management Development and is a Fellow of the Chartered Institute of Personnel and Development (UK).

John is widely published. *New Role, New Reality* (2000) was short-listed as book of the year by the U.S. Society of Human Resource Management. *Leaders Must Lead!* (2003) reached #3 on one best-seller list. *Myth, Magic, Mindset: A template for organizational culture change* (2008) is in its third printing. *Without Breaking Stride* (2009) is being used internationally.

For permission to use any of the questionnaires included in the book, in your own organization, including the Culture Work-Up, please contact John Burdett at orxestra@rogers.com.

ORXESTRA INC.